# SOCIAL CAPITAL-ISM

## For Historical Understanding Of Climate Change Economics

Bob Ticer

Copyright © 2019   Bobby Dee Ticer

All rights reserved

ISBN: 978-1-797404-40-0

Printed by Kindle Print, An Amazon.com Company

## ACKNOWLEDGEMENTS

There has been a tremendous effort to combat climate change by countless experts and concerned citizens. This book is merely a continuation of the effort by means of a historic perspective of political economic development from early civilization.

## CONTENTS

1. INTRODUCTION — 1
2. NATURAL CYCLES OR INDUSTRIAL CAUSE OF CLIMATE CHANGE — 7
3. SOLUTIONS FOR REVERSING CLIMATE CHANGE — 14
4. RISE OF CIVILIZATION — 26
5. POLITICAL ECONOMIC HISTORY OF EUROPE — 35
6. DEMOCRATIC REPUBLIC AMERICA — 43
7. BANK AMERICA — 48
8. SLAVERY CONTROVERSY AND CIVIL WAR — 53
9. CHANGE AND ADJUSTMENT ECONOMICS — 59
10. INFLATION DEFLATION ECONOMICS — 68
11. LAW AND ORDER OF MONETARY FREEDOM — 76
12. FINANCING ECONOMIC CLIMATE CHANGE — 84

1

# INTRODUCTION

The term Social Capitalism might seem to be a contradiction in the sense capitalism generally connotes free choice for individual innovation to achieve economic success. However, there are many social aspects of economics that are complementary to individual determination of it. They are generally less acknowledged than is freedom of choice.

There is social tax for the construction of roads and highways for more efficient transportation of goods and services. Although they promote prosperity for both the rich and poor of us because of more transport of goods and services, there is an advantage for more wealthy individuals or corporations to use them, as it is cheaper on the average to transport goods in larger bulk whereby fewer owners capitalize on their profit. Those of us who can afford large trucks, warehouses and so forth are more capable of capitalizing on their efficiency of use. For instance, there were gasoline wars in the 1950s. Although the price of gasoline was lowered to nineteen cents a gallon, such major oil companies as Shell were able to eliminate competition of smaller companies by selling at lower prices. However, they were also able to raise prices afterwards even higher with the elimination of competitors.

A progressive tax of the wealthier of us thus seems reasonable in order for a fairer distribution of wealth among us. It is not that we do not deserve the opportunity to become wealthy; rather, it is only that we should not become wealthy at the expense of increasing poverty that is of issue, as an unbalanced distribution of wealth is a contributing factor for a stagnant economy that can be detrimental to both the rich and poor, as to eliminate customers for goods and services.

A central principle of economics is supply and demand. A greater ratio of supply to its demand is claimed to generally lower the price of goods. However, there is also a cost factor relating to the number of competitors. Too many of them could result in them selling cheaper instead of them using innovation for better quality of product, which could be unaffordable because of more expense for less demand. Sears used to have a reputation for high quality products. With the addition of foreign competition producing cheaper products of less quality, Sears has been closing many of its stores. However, although some sellers profit from misleading advertising, there are still a great number of companies, such as tire and hardware stores that maintain a favorable reputation regarding quality products and excellent services.

Regarding the open market, farms selling apples competing with farms selling oranges could render too much production cost for each farm. Regarding politics, two similar candidates could divide votes for both of them to lose to a less popular third candidate. Regarding governmental facilities, an electric and water utility can operate more efficiently above cost if selling to more customers. However, to the contrary, the public utility could raise prices by it being a monopoly if not controlled by public scrutiny in voting for public officials.

A fundamental negative of free enterprise is that competition of it can lead to a single winner, wherefrom it becomes less free. It is recognized as either monopoly or oligopoly. Although they are supposedly opposed by governmental authorities of a democracy of free enterprise, the wealthier among us still have an advantage inasmuch as they can afford more extensive coverage of the news media, advertise product, contribute more to the election of officials, and thereby lobby more effectively. Such advantages can even affect our health and general well-being. Although doctors heal and save lives, they also have expenses of education and so forth for them to profit more on medicine than for allowing natural cures, as to prescribe opioids promoted by lobbying that are unknowingly addictive of heroin to have led to countless deaths.

There are both positive and negative consequences of advertising. In the 1950s there was such advertising of shampoos for the prevention of dandruff. A cousin of mine shampooed three times a week. Her hair was completely white before she turned forty. In contrast, I heard from a teacher that shampooing washes out natural oils. I then hardly ever washed my hair for it to have plenty of color still in my seventies. However, it started to turn gray in my early fifties. The color came back when I consumed nutritional supplements. I have since simply consumed a more nutritional diet at the expense of doctors for little or no need of their services.

A counterargument is that beauty is in the eye of the beholder whereby it is our responsibility to determine what is acceptable for our own needs. Those of us who choose wisely are more likely to succeed in life. If we all choose wisely, then it would likely promote innovation for better product. However, what is right for one consumer can be wrong for another consumer. Smoking cigarettes can lead to cancer, but some people smoke them while living a healthy life for about a hundred years or more, as a late World War II veteran drank alcohol and smoked cigars and still lived to be one-hundred and six years of age, which the advancement of medicine and doctor services could very well have attributed to a general increase in average life. However, for what I know, most of my relatives who smoked cigarettes died of cancer. Even though they died of cancer, they craved smoking so much they detested government advertising attempting to discourage them of their freedom to smoke. The one exception was my father who quit when he was in his forties and lived to be ninety-three.

The issues are complex and the science is not always totally correct. Statistics might indicate consuming too much sugar leads to poor health, but they do not prove sugar alone is the cause, as the single cause might be a combination of sugar with other dietary elements. For instance, the total cause might be too much sugar along with dehydration, as water can help flush out toxic elements and the oxygen in water might provide more lasting energy by combining with carbon of sugar, as in contrast to the immediate energy of air with it having an oxygen nitrogen balance. Although this is merely speculation, it is still possible future knowledge might be such that it recognizes more complex combinations of nutrients whereby a little more sugar in a balanced diet could promote more energy on occasion. For instance, I felt healthier after I began adding a little ginger to my oats. The healthier feeling could have been coincidence or the ginger might have improved my digestion enough to absorb other nutrients I had needed to process the conversion of oxygen and carbon to carbon monoxide.

A more general principle for favorable results of life experiences relates to balance. The air we breathe contains mostly oxygen and nitrogen. Oxygen is more volatile while nitrogen is more of a container allowing for the flow of energy. Balance is needed, as too much of an ingredient can be detrimental to health. As balance, air provides us with quick energy to keep us going. On the other hand, the oxygen in water combining with hydrogen, carbon and other elements is stored energy within us for more extensive activity. If health statistics on the consumption of sugar do not include dehydration effects, then the results could be incomplete. However, too much of anything is not good. Too much competition of deciding between apples and oranges for each to have less demand could render their cost too expensive to produce. Even too much balance is not good. For instance, a balanced budget during a particular situation could be a negative factor in maintaining a stagnant economy needing more monetary credit for investment.

There are nonetheless helpful indications of knowledge to acknowledge. I grew up on a sugar diet, adding more sugar to cereal that already contained it. I had little stamina. After consuming a little sugar at work, I felt less energetic a half-hour later. However, disregarding there being less allergic pollens in the air, I seemed to have more energy during the hotter part of the summer when I drank more water. Afterwards, I only drank water while working a ten-hour shift without getting tired, whereas coworkers who consumed sweets during break times appeared to be exhausted at the end of the shift even though they worked slower and produced fewer products. However, with an improved diet, I now drink soda pop once in a while to have more immediate energy. Sometimes the result seems positive; sometimes they seem negative. Regarding the latter, I tend to gas more after drinking the soda pop to have heartburn. Regarding the former, x-rays were unable to detect the kidney stone after I drank soda pop for a week, and after doctors had told me my kidney stone was too big to pass on out of my body.

Although science is not always correct, that does not mean it does not lead to a more comprehensive understanding of reality. Doctors still save lives and cure us of our ailments, and science has contributed enormously to the invention of technological advances in numerous products. It is only when they interfere with our freedom of choice that they become politically or theoretically controversial.

More political challenge is regarding environmental issues. For instance, in some areas of the state of New Mexico where water supply is limited, local government allows one water-well per lot. The land has far less value on the average. Land purchasers from afar, who have been enticed by the low price of lots, as advertised as available real estate, end up not paying the tax required for its ownership for them to forfeit the land to the local government that resells it at the cheaper price in maintaining tax revenue.

To the contrary is the need to protect the water supply for the common needs of the people. Situations are circumstantially complex. In some cases, it is the sole responsibility of the individual to determine the outcome; in other cases, it is the responsibility of government to protect the needs of the general public. The underlying principle here considered is that we as individuals live our lives as we see fit, but that when less desirable circumstances are too much for individuals to overcome by themselves, then social unity as majority rule can be a more successful means of overcoming them.

Social policy of government has been referred to as Social Democracy. Critics of it often refer to it as simply socialism, whereas Social Democracy in such countries as Sweden is considered by them as a complement to free enterprise. The term Social Capitalism is more of a direct approach for understanding the interrelation between social and individual aspects of capitalism. It can be subcategorized: such as, government and law and order are needed to protect the economic wealth of capitalism; government investment in railroads, highways, etc., help promote capitalism; government favoring other product for environmental concerns competes with free enterprise. Regarding the latter, combating climate change needs to be shown as economically feasible as is free enterprise in order to help it overcome its denial.

The intent here is not merely to change terminology. It is for more individual understanding for how we can succeed in life by individual choice to conform to social needs by either political vote or economic purchase of product. Social Democracy mainly refers to such governmental entitlements as Social Security, parks, roads and so forth. Social Capitalism here refers to the complex entanglement of how social and individual needs of the economy interrelate.

Pool shooters who plan their strategy and know how to implement it are generally more successful at winning. The more they know the more options they have on the table in being more creative at implementing their plan. In principle, education and the advancement of knowledge has provided more ways to success. As a social aspect of Democracy, the USA was the first to provide free education as a right for all of us to be able to achieve more in life for all of us to capitalize on. The result has been more knowledgeable competition for greater innovation of more advanced products.

More understanding of climate change is here attempted by means of reviewing the historical development of modern civilization apart from political denial of its prejudice. Politicians tend to inform voters what they want to hear. Even if climate change is a greater threat to humanity and overall wealth of the economy, and even if climatologists are thorough in their assessment of it as man-caused, politicians still tend to deny it publicly as such. It is their goal to become elected to office whereas the goal here is to pursue a better understanding of truth for the possibility of a more livable planet with more opportunity of prosperity along with peace and tranquility.

The understanding begins with a critique on climate change. I once said I wrote a booklet on pool but did not read it. The claim sounded humorous, but a poetic connotation of it is that you see more of yourself if you look in the mirror. If you read more of what you write, you find errors and begin to realize more of what you do not know, as in putting together a jigsaw puzzle and seeing the picture that emerges. Being critical is not merely to refute; it is a means of obtaining a more complete understanding of reality. That is to say it is more difficult to learn in some situations if you believe you already know everything. Challenging what you do not know just to be able to understand it instead of bias denial of it can be self-educational. Even regarding science, challenging theories of the establishment, even if they are wrong, often promote theory by contriving experiments to confirm one or the other.

There is thus a critique on climate change. It is not merely to change the minds of deniers of it; it is also to reveal more options of how to combat it.

Following the critique on climate change is a review for remedies to combat and even reverse it. However, many of the solutions need to overcome economic politics. Thus, following is a review of the historical rise of civilization regarding the political development of economics.

The political development of economics commences with the development of agriculture that allowed for such construction as large pyramids, but led to more competition for wealth that often resulted in wars between nations. Free enterprise of a more laisse-faire economics developed in Europe in replacing Physiocratic and Mercantile economics mainly of France and England. The economic development continued with the rise of the United States of America along with its maintaining of unity after the Civil War and the Great Depression of the 1930s.

Although modern day economics of free enterprise developed in Europe, there are still social consequences of it regarding periods of recession and depression of the economy that still occur. Still, from this historical review, it is to become evident how such social remedies regarding environmental concerns can contribute to having more prosperity along with a more peaceful environment. The economics is thus further analyzed in the context of how both freedom of choice and social conformity can contribute to its success.

We sometimes fear what we do not know. Some of us fear not climate change as much as government interference in our daily lives. However, the understanding of climate change and how applicable remedies can enhance both our living conditions for more prosperity and freedom could become more of an acceptable and conforming goal of life. There is already effort in place for this understanding. The effort here is merely to build on it because of the tremendous effort that is still needed for all of us to contribute. Here, the effort continues with an analysis of climate change and a historical understanding of the social and economic development of our modern-day civilization.

# 2

# NATURAL CYCLES

# OR

# INDUSTRIAL CAUSE OF CLIMATE CHANGE

A previous belief of climatologists was that the average yearly temperature of Earth had been constant for millions of years. That belief was challenged by geophysicist and astronomer Milutin Milankovic hypothesizing that changes in how Earth revolves around the Sun results in more extensive temperature cycles than those merely of seasonal changes. One extensive cycle factor he theorized includes such influences of other planets, particularly of Jupiter and Saturn, on Earth's orbit around the Sun. More influential is two changes in Earth's axial tilt: one being a change in the amount of axial tilt occurring at a particular time of year, which is about a twenty-six-thousand-year cycle; the other being how the amount of tilt occurring in the twenty-six-thousand-year cycle, which is about a forty-thousand-year cycle. Also included in climate analyses is the geographical difference whereby more surface water exists in the southern hemisphere than in the northern hemisphere. Insulating factors and the chemistry of how different elements absorb and emit heat are also included.

It had been reasoned that a constant yearly temperature results from all of Earth receiving the same amount of heat from the Sun per year. However, even though the yearly distance of Earth from the Sun is nearly the same now than it was millions of years ago, the amount of time when Earth is nearer or farther from the Sun does change temporarily from the influence of the other planets in the solar system, as their gravitational pull on Earth counters the Sun's gravitational pull on Earth.

The constancy of yearly sunlight is according to Kepler's laws of orbital motion of the planets around the Sun. By Kepler's first law the Earth's orbit around the Sun is an ellipse, which differs from a circle in that it has two foci instead of a center. The location of the Sun is one of the foci whereby Earth's surface area receives more sunlight per distance squared when closer to the Sun. However, by Kepler's second law of planetary motion, the orbital time when Earth is closer to the Sun is proportionately less because of an increase in speed-squared than when it is farther away. Because area per time between the Sun and Earth counters the average of time squared per distance, their opposite effects on the average nullify each other.

Average distance of Earth from the Sun along the ellipse is still the same as the radius of a circle for Earth to still receive the same amount of sunlight per year. However, the positional influence of other planets temporary alters the eccentricity of Earth's orbit around the Sun. The ellipses of the planets around the Sun vary in distances and speeds. When either Saturn or Jupiter is closer to Earth than at other times, Earth is more accelerated towards them when approaching closer to them. After closest approach, the process reverses for Earth to decelerate more from them while closer. Earth's distance from the Sun is thus momentarily increased during the additional rates of acceleration and deceleration for it to receive less sunlight than in another yearly cycle.

Because the amount of sunlight Earth receives from the Sun partly depends on the location of other planets also having gravitational influence on the orbit of Earth around the Sun, they generally balance out with complex cycles. Earth's orbital ellipse is also nearly that of a circle.

A more influential cycle is that of Earth's axial tilt. At the present time, the Antarctica tilt towards the Sun during its summer is when Earth is closer to the Sun, whereas the Arctic summer tilt towards the Sun is when Earth is farther from the Sun. Even though the Antarctica tilt away from the Sun is of a colder winter because of it being father away from the sun than the Arctic is during its winter, there is a warming trend per year because of the greater water surface of the southern atmosphere being able to absorb and retain more summer heat than does the northern atmosphere. The difference in summer heat is simply greater than the difference in winter heat.

Although the amount of sunlight all of Earth receives per year is still constant, the containment of sunlight energy varies at different locations. Because there is more surface water in the southern hemisphere, it absorbs more of the Sun's heat instead of allowing it to reflect or be emitted back into space than does the greater land surface in the northern hemisphere. All of Earth on the average thus tends to be warmer because of Antarctica being closer to the Sun during its summer time than that of the northern hemisphere being closer to the Sun during its summertime. However, the twenty-six-thousand-year cycle, approximately, is reversing in about the next thirteen-thousand years for a tendency of the present ice age to become colder because of Earth's tilt in the northern hemisphere towards the sun becoming more when Earth is closer to the Sun than it is during winter time, whereby there is less surface water for retaining the summer heat. (There is also difference in total ocean surface when glaciers of ice buildup for the sea level to have been lower between two-hundred and three-hundred feet, as the glaciers nearer to the poles receive less light to melt by absorbing heat.)

Earth should also have been cooler about thirteen thousand years ago when its northern hemisphere was closer to the sun. However, the difference in summer and winter temperatures would also have been more severe and volatile. With all the glaciers aided by the colder winters, the hotter summers of more surface water from melting of snow and ice would absorb more heat, and less plant life from the cold would absorb less carbon dioxide from the atmosphere.

It is generally realized that change in weather, as for different seasons, is mostly the result of Earth's axial tilt than its distance from the Sun. At present, Earth is closest to the Sun during January; it is farthest from the Sun during July. Earth's average distance from the Sun is about ninety-three million miles. Its closest distance to the Sun is about ninety-one million and one-hundred thousand miles. Its farthest distance is about ninety-four million and eight-hundred thousand miles. The ratio of difference in distance to average distance is about one-twenty-fifth compared to its ratio of axial tile of less than one-eighth: about twenty degrees tilt from one-hundred and eighty. The ratio of axial tilt is almost four times as great for more direct sunlight. The direction of tilt could thus have greater effect. Eventually, the longer days nearer to the northern Summer Solstice will be when Earth is closest to the Sun for a tendency of respective summers and winters to become even hotter and colder in the northern hemisphere even though the yearly temperature of all Earth should be cooler.

The degree of Earth's axial tilt also changes in about a forty-thousand-year cycle. Since the tilt is now becoming less, Earth again should be cooling even faster similar to the same reason as before: less ratio of summer heat in the southern hemisphere to that in the northern hemisphere because of less magnitude of summer heat during the Arctic summer. However, evidence is to the contrary, as the average temperature of water at the equator has been increasing according to climatologists.

Other natural factors contributing to climate change are volcanic eruptions and large meteors. The probability of them occurring declines with those of greater magnitude, but their effects are nonetheless evident. As noted by Benjamin Franklin, the winters in both Europe and the United States were abnormally colder after an eruption occurred on Iceland in 1782. During a period of about eight months of volcanic activity the atmosphere was filled with volcanic ash to interfere with the sun's radiation. Climate was also cooler after an eruption of Mount Saint Helens in the state of Washington in 1980.

An eruption at El Chichn, Mexico occurred in 1982 that had almost five times the cooling effect of Mount Saint Helens. Although the El Chichn eruption had a smaller ash cloud, it contained much more sulfuric acid particles that remained suspended in the atmosphere longer to absorb and either reflect or emit sunlight back into outer space.

There are also natural warming factors. Natural coal fires have existed for millennia, as in Wyoming and Western North Dakota. What was once believed to be a volcano on the Australian Burning Mountain is now known to be a coal fire that has been burning for about six-thousand years. The natural coal fires result in the atmosphere absorbing carbon dioxide from them in what is now scientifically evident as a warming factor.

Somewhat more speculative is the chemical complexity of how heat determines the nature of matter. Water can absorb a tremendous amount of heat, as demonstrated by boiling water in a paper cup placed in a campfire, but water will fuel a grease fire instead of smothering it. Snow and ice are of low temperature, but they are also insulators not preventing their containment to become even colder. Eskimos lived in igloos made of ice to shelter their warmer bodies from the outside cold.

Further effects are the reduction of plant life. Less plant life absorbs less carbon dioxide from the atmosphere for there to be a tendency of a warmer temperature. As colder water absorbs instead the carbon dioxide from the atmosphere, more animate life is created to produce even more carbon dioxide. Too much consumption of plant life thus tends to warm Earth. To compensate, animal life could consume other animal life instead of plant life. However, too much plant life with less animal life could also lead to a colder Earth.

Wind and water currents are also factors. Although much of North America, Europe and northern Asia areas were once buried beneath miles of glacial ice, a warm water current from the equator to the North Pole warmed coast lines of even more land allowed by sea levels being at the time about three hundred feet lower than they are now. There was a land bridge between Asia and Alaska for migration of people down the Pacific Coast to South America, as indicated by controversial evidence, to be more than forty thousand years ago.

Although glaciers of ice sheets covered land more inland from the seas, ice and snow are also insulators from colder below their freezing temperature. Eskimos have survived in igloos as ice shelters in Alaska. They penetrated into waters below ice to live on fish. Such large animals as mammoths could also have benefited by breathing a more energetic air having more oxygen and less carbon dioxide, as indicated by trapped air pockets of the past.

The present concern of climatologists is a change to the carbon cycle of the atmosphere. It is claimed that more carbon dioxide in the atmosphere results in higher humidity for absorbing more heat, as from either sunlight or lower energy microwaves that move every which way through space with no common origin. Although the South Pole now tilts closer to the Sun during summer for more absorption of heat, and although the axial tilt of Earth is reversing during the next thirteen-thousand years for a colder tendency of Earth's climate, more carbon dioxide in the atmosphere not only counters the freeze, as would occur in the winter months, the summers in the northern hemisphere might tend to become warmer because of its tilt towards the Sun during summertime when closer to the Sun. Sometime in the faraway future, Canada could benefit with a warmer summer and longer growing season, even though it could also have a colder winter. In contrast, the United States could be much warmer in the summer than it is now for more desert and need of air conditioning. Although it is dryness that results in desert instead of directly from heat, the temperature in the arid climate of Death Valley in the Mojave Desert of California was once recorded as one-hundred and twenty-four degrees Fahrenheit, second only to one-hundred and twenty-six degrees Fahrenheit recorded in the Sahara Desert of Northern Africa. However, water absorbs more heat, just at a lower temperature, as temperature is a particular magnitude of the quantity of heat instead of the magnitude of heat itself. Higher temperature thus does not necessarily mean more heat. However, heat of a higher temperature substance does tend to flow to heat of a lower temperature substance.

Global Warming of climate change can seem doubtful in view of freezing winters, but extreme cold can also result from warming. To understand the cause, consider why island temperature near the equator remains mostly constant, as ideal around seventy degrees Fahrenheit. It is partly because daytime and nighttime remain nearly the same year around close to the equator, partly because more water contains more heat at a lower temperature, and partly because a large amount of ocean water within the tropical area is absorbed more by the warmer air. Since water consists of hydrogen, which is the smallest atom, the warmer humid air of water vapor, as gas, is lighter for it to be pushed up to a higher altitude by the denser-dryer air. As the moist air at the equator arises, it leaves a vacuum for dryer air of trade winds from the directions of the poles to replace it. As a result, the latitudes between the equator and poles thus tend to receive more of the cold air from the poles because of there being more of the hotter air rising at the equator.

Coastal areas are normally of milder temperatures than are farther inland conditions. However, they are also more vulnerable to hurricanes and sometimes flooding that result from changes in temperature of a vast amount of stored energy over large surface areas of oceans. The winds become greater and more destructive as Earth becomes hotter with its variance in temperature.

More extreme hurricanes originate from the equator, as to move up the Atlantic Ocean to mostly the USA and anything in its way to offset the more extreme cold coming from the direction of the North Pole. The cause is complex. When the warm ocean water near the equator evaporates into a gas, the ocean loses both heat and water. The more humid air results in chemical reactions. There is an electrical attraction for condensation into rainclouds. Centers of attraction, as eyes of the storm, are also present, whereby they become surrounded by the swirling of hot humid air that is lighter and easier for them to swirl away from the equator towards the poles. With more heat from the oceans they, on the average, become more volatile and/or larger for causing wind destruction and flooding. There is also the counter of colder arctic flowing toward the equator to replace other dryer air replacing the rise of more humid air.

Why the air is hotter, as claimed by climatologists, is due to the excessive use of fossil fuel being released into the atmosphere. There is an equilibrium state of balance known as the carbon cycle. Carbon, C, is needed for the growth of food and other essentials. As part of this carbon cycle, we breathe in air for oxygen, which can be toxic if the air contains too much of it. We breathe out carbon monoxide, CO, which is normally too toxic to breathe back into our lungs. The CO soon absorbs more O from the air for it to convert into carbon dioxide, $CO_2$. It is far less toxic to breathe, but it results in the atmosphere absorbing more radiant heat because of a greater molecular bondage to separate it, and too much carbon in the atmosphere results in an average rise in temperature of the atmosphere.

The carbon in the atmosphere also bonds with hydrogen from water molecules for a greater humidity potential absorbing even more heat and water. Although more humid air absorbs more heat than the carbon alone does, the carbon also allows the air to absorb more water. (Carbon is unique in that it can bond indefinitely with itself and other atoms for more combinations of elements.) It is still the greater humidity allowed by the $CO_2$ as the main contributor to global warming.

Our livelihoods depend on the carbon cycle. We need carbon for food. We need oxygen to breathe. At the other end of the cycle is plant life absorbing $CO_2$ from the air and releasing oxygen back into the atmosphere. There can thus be a balance between the use of carbon fuel and plant life for an equilibrium state of existence. However, if too much of the dormant state of carbon is mined for fuel, and deforestation occurs as well, then the equilibrium state of the atmosphere is increased to a toxic level.

Great bodies of water, as the oceans, are a carbon sink. They provide sea life with food, but too much $CO_2$ absorbed by water can also acidity it too much for sustaining ocean life. As oceans become warmer, they contain and absorb less $CO_2$, while remaining more acid.

Conditions are expected to become even worse in the future. It is thus evident more remedies of climate change are needed, as to both adjust to it and reverse it. There are remedies, but there is an entanglement of the economy to overcome in order for them to be implemented.

The cost of climate change can be expensive, as for its damage to property and life, preparing for its negative effects, and altering its future effects. Such cost of climate change itself could be much more than the cost of reversing it. How such cost for the reversal of it can be paid for is now the issue to be more adequately understood. However, to promote it, the remedies themselves need to be more understood as such, including education of it and so forth.

Natural climate change in addition to polluting the atmosphere with hydrocarbon fuels is more complex. What is needed is more investment in climatology to determine future effects of weather to determine remedies for such possible catastrophes as severe times of cold and heat, hurricanes, tornadoes, flooding, extensive forest fires, extreme drought and so forth. Physics and chemistry are also essential for knowledge, which itself provides more viable options to either counter or prepare adverse effects of future weather.

# 3

# SOLUTIONS

# FOR

# REVERSING CLIMATE CHANGE

The human cause of climate change is claimed by scientologists to be the mining for hydrocarbon fuels from within Earth's surface that needs to be replaced by plant life that has been reduced by human caused deforestation. Proposed remedies for Climate Change thus include an increase in plant life along with more use of solar energy in place of carbon fuels.

Most solar energy replacing carbon fuels is solar panels converting sunlight into electricity. Solar wind also converts to electricity, and electric vehicles to replace the use of gasoline are becoming a viable option. Still, the effects of Climate Change are becoming more evident, as measure of average temperature of ocean water at the equator has increased along with such effects as more frequent and disastrous hurricanes. Record flooding in 2017 from hurricanes caused billions of dollars of damage in Texas, along with human lives, and the subsequent flooding in 2018 resulted in human deaths and destroyed countless homes and other property worth billions of dollars. Record wildfires in California have spread more easily from greater heat and wind in causing billions of dollars of damage along with human life, and the subsequent flooding in 2018 destroyed countless homes along with human life. Record low temperatures in northern parts of the United States have caused more deaths and the cancel of flights from major airports along with too hazardous conditions on roads for driving automobiles on them. The excessive strain of electric utilities was also a strain on people being forced to bear hazardous conditions of colder weather. The number of influenza cases also doubled in 2018, which is believed to relate to the acidity conditions of warmer water and humid air from too much carbon producing heat.

Climate change remedies are doable. Solar panels and electric vehicles have become more affordable and practical. Solar energy and reforestation counter the carbon pollution of the atmosphere.

However, they by themselves are only partial remedies not expected to reverse climate change, as is now needed, since more trees die and decay along with more forest fires to reverse their carbon absorption.

Some remedies that have been proposed for reversing climate change include carbon capture, reversing ocean acidity by adding iron to it, and spraying sulfuric acid into the air. However, they are generally too speculative as of yet with the possibility of having disastrous side effects.

An advanced air scrubber for carbon capture was proposed in 2009 by physicist Peter Eisenberger, and it became supported by his colleague Graciela Chichilnisky, who had become educated in economics and mathematics. Although air scrubbers had already been established in power plants, over half of $CO_2$ emissions come from such smaller emissions as automobiles, farms and houses. Although the outside air contains only about one part of $CO_2$ per two-hundred and fifty parts of air, the Einsenberger method uses steam as a lower temperature for cost efficiency. Chichilnisky advocated the capture of $CO_2$ be sold to such established users of it as resupplying oil wells and making carbonated beverages. A commercial plant to collect $CO_2$ from the air was operational in Switzerland in 2017, and plants in New York of the USA were planned for 2018 along with several other plants elsewhere. The plant in Switzerland sold the $CO_2$ to a nearby greenhouse for increasing the growth of plants for even more absorption of carbon with the release of oxygen back into the atmosphere.

It should also be noted that, in 2008, David Keith built structure four feet wide with a twenty-foot height having a fan at its bottom for sucking in air. The air came out of the top with less than half as much $CO_2$ it had entered with. He also suggested spraying sulfuric acid into the lower stratosphere at the equator for winds to distribute it around the globe to reflect sunlight back into outer space. However, the side effects are not adequately understood as of yet, such as possible depletion of the ozone layer, resulting weather patterns around Earth, and how to reverse the long-time accumulation of too much of the gas being emitted in the stratosphere from possible error of calculation from lack of knowledge.

David Keith, who became president of a company named Carbon Engineering, has claimed it will be economically feasible in 2021 to produce gasoline from limestone, hydrogen and air by means of a vast network of air scrubbers. Although it will not itself reduce the amount of carbon in the atmosphere, it will not result in its increase.

Dispersing iron into ocean water was tried as somewhat more of a careless but successful speculation. It had become evident that ocean life is decreasing due to the acidity of too much $CO_2$, but not enough carbon was evident in colder waters. In 1992, a collapse of the Newfoundland cod fishery occurred. Too much fishing was blamed for its cause. However, in 2008, a volcano erupted on the Aleutian Islands to spread volcanic ash over the Gulf of Alaska. An unusually massive bloom of phytoplankton was noticed after a few months and a 2010 Frazer River run of sockeye salmon followed, which was followed again in 2011 by about six million of them. The result indicated that the number of salmon in the ocean can be increased with an iron supplement.

Against international law, the disapproval of scientists and the ire of environmentalists, Russ George along with the Haida Salmon Restoration Corporation conducted an experiment in 2012 to spread one-hundred tons of iron sulfate over an ocean eddy about three-hundred miles from the Queen Charlotte Islands of Canada. Phytoplankton formed months later within about a one-hundred-kilometer area, followed in 2013 by about four times as much pink salmon.

As Ken Whitehead explained it, in his article titled A Dangerous Experiment Gone Right, there tends to be a warm layer of ocean water over the deep colder water. There lacks a mixing of nutrients because of this division, which is necessary for a healthy marine environment. Phytoplankton needs iron for photosynthesis from the atmosphere for acquiring inorganic carbon. More $CO_2$ is then absorbed for the dead cells of phytoplankton to sink to the ocean bottom, and for allowing more collection of carbon from the atmosphere.

Although the experiment appears to have been successful, more caution is still advised regarding the balance of nature. Although the algae blooms of phytoplankton increase at a rapid rate from the photosynthesis of sunlight and absorbing of nitrogen and phosphorous (as from iron), too much blooming also appears to starve fish of needed oxygen, and some types of algae are poisonous. Scientific studies are thus still needed for a continuous application of the procedure.

Another promising remedy of climate change is the production of an agriculturally charcoal fertilizer now known as bio-char. Whether knowledgeable or simply the usual way of farming and cooking at the time, it is evident that such practices produced enough bio-char to fertilize the infertile soils of the Amazon about two-thousand years ago. They are still more fertile than neighboring soils to this day.

In modern times, farmers burn after their growing season to fertilize the soil for next season. Similarly, forest fires not large enough to destroy the forest contribute to soil fertility for the growth of more trees. Bio-char is simply a conversion of hydrocarbons to a fertile charcoal. The process of producing it is to separate it from oxygen and heat it in a range of about between seven-hundred-and-nine-hundred degrees Fahrenheit. Generally, a small flame at the top of a container burns a small amount of the carbon fuel while most of the heat sinks below to transform non-fertile carbon into fertile carbon.

The benefits of bio-char are not only that it enhances production of healthy food; there is less carbon added to the atmosphere. If forest waste is used to produce it, it could result in less forest fires and more controllable ones, saving billions of dollars per year while assisting in the control of climate change.

Bio-char is simply a faster transformation of compost. Sawdust, for instance, can become effective compost after about two years of being a ground cover. It first absorbs fertile nitrogen from the soil and then gradually releases it back into the soil along with fertile carbon. Bio-char itself is about seventy percent carbon with the rest of it being mostly of nitrogen, hydrogen and oxygen elements. It benefits the soil mainly by it absorbing, retaining and purifying water along with its fertilization. There is a nitrogen cycle whereby the chemical diversity of the bio-char allows microbiological organs to process the nitrogen of infertile nitrate to a fertile nitrate. It can be combined with other compost for even healthier results depending on the particular condition of the soil and what is to be grown. However, too much nitrate can be harmful, as to promote poisonous algae.

A key condition relating to the combating of climate change is that of balance. It is not that the use of carbon is itself wrong; it is too much use of carbon in a way it pollutes the atmosphere that is wrong. Similarly, not enough consumption of vitamin A (carotene) can result in us having blindness, baldness and even death; too much vitamin A in the human diet can also result in blindness, baldness and death.

Balance can be a key to success, but it is also conditional in the sense that some of us might require more of it than others. Remedies for both the natural cause and manmade cause of climate change are thus more complex. Science is needed for more of its future understanding.

What is to be understood regarding balance of climate change is mainly how too much heat energy becomes stored in the atmosphere, and how it can be changed. Heat is energy that can convert into other forms of it. An effective means of reversing global warming is simply to use the heat in a way that it does not immediately recycle back to heat. For instance, it can be converted to electricity and so forth after it converts to wind from air exchanging temperature with other air. The electricity could provide enough pressure to produce such carbon products as carbon steel and commercial diamonds whereby the carbon used need not be readily decomposed for it to be absorbed into the atmosphere as heat. Moreover, commercial diamonds could be used to produce diamond batteries. Batteries of miniature diamonds are now claimed to be able to last as long as five-hundred years. Heat energy can thus be transformed into another form of energy that can be contained for hundreds of years.

There has been a great amount of effort put forth to reverse global warming. The effort has mostly been socially political. On the federal level, tax credits have been proposed for the purchase of electric vehicles. Water and electric utilities on state and country levels have offered to purchase electricity from home owners who produce it by way of solar panels. The utilities are also receiving electricity from wind turbines sponsored by such states as California and Oregon. On the individual level is the use of bicycles, the purchase of electric vehicles and the growth of plant life that absorbs more carbon dioxide from the atmosphere.

How such joint effort can be successful is indicative of the construction of the Grand Coulee dam in the state of Washington. It allowed for farming along with power to generate electricity to develop, in turn, a prosperous community. To the contrary, a severe drought in Afghanistan has resulted in farmers growing opium to survive, and to become controlled by drug dealers and terrorists. Similar results have become routine in poor areas of Mexico and other less developed countries where drug lords have gained control.

How water can be stored and used is a vital means of reversing climate change. It relates to Beaver Engineering. The engineering and construction of canals and irrigation systems had previously coincided with the rise of civilization in the Mesopotamian Valley and elsewhere. The Assyrian empire of the ninth century BC appears to have been the first to construct a long-distance canal system of sophisticated aqueducts that expanded the range of farming. The Babylonians followed suit a century later, and Jerusalem did likewise after another century for water to flow over a bridge nearly a thousand meters wide and through a tunnel more than five-hundred meters long. Also, during that century, Greeks constructed aqueducts to supply the Greece cities Athens and Samos with drinking water.

Roman aqueduct construction began in the third century BC. It was promoted by an invention of an arch and a large-scale inverted siphon of clay or lead pipes, which were reinforced with stone blocks to allow water to flow on a large-scale straighter path by means of gravity and water pressure. Even more scientific innovation allowed for more tunneling for underground aqueducts and water reservoirs that extended hundreds of miles from Rome. The Roman Empire even extended its construction of them to other countries.

These past accomplishments are merely an indication of how remedies of climate change are possible by commitment. A great number of people and organizations of this modern time have already committed to it. The purchase of solar panels and electric cars are by individual choice. Such other remedies unaffordable by individuals, such as methods to abstract water from the atmosphere, require more of a social remedy, as of government and/or participation of large corporations for financing them.

There are now many remedies to climate change on the open market. Solar panels have become affordable and have been promoted by water and electric utilities in some states. Electric cars are now a viable option to purchase, and they are being promoted by such countries as China and Germany. Non-explosive lithium batteries to travel three-hundred miles or more without recharging are now available. There is a small toy car for my nephew's three-year-old son to ride that is cheaper than other batteries, and it operates for seventeen hours before needing to be recharged. I purchased a long time ago a flashlight that still works without battery replacement.

Other remedies are too expensive for most individuals to purchase. Although alcohol has been used as a fuel throughout history, such as an early source for engine combustion, and ethanol is now produced from corn in the Midwest, alcohol fuel along with electric batteries has been replaced mostly with gasoline engines. The cause is mainly that of convenience. Even though ethanol has a greater octane rating for more efficiency than gasoline does, ethanol has less combustive energy than gasoline and is more difficult to ignite in colder weather. Even the mixture of ethanol with gasoline is inconvenient. The mixture requires about ninety-five percent pure alcohol. However, such inconveniences can be overcome with the use of an alcohol now known as biobutanol.

Biobutanol has an energy density close to that of gasoline, and it has a twenty-five cent better octane rating than gasoline, but it requires more chemical knowledge to effectively produce it as an economic alternative. It combines with gasoline and diesel fuels in allowing more water in the mixture than does ethanol. There are now technological claims that it can be produced from any green plants by solar energy and such fermentation bacteria as that from zebra waste.

Besides using solar energy to abstract heat from the atmosphere, the water vapor mostly containing it can also be abstracted. There are methods to abstract water from the atmosphere even in arid climates, but they are neither affordable nor cost effective for most individuals.

Water itself is a main factor linking other factors of climate change. Biomass, such as dead wood in forest is a fire hazard. It can be collected as another energy source, being either burned directly or converted into bio-char if cooked at seven-hundred degrees Fahrenheit in a container with little or no oxygen. Oil companies also pump out about seven times more water from the ground than oil. Although the water is mostly saline, it still can be useful, as for putting out forest fires and the growth of food in semi-arid areas. A massive storage of it underground or in containers shielding it from sunlight could be prosperous for a greenhouse production of food or simply absorption of carbon from the atmosphere.

Surface water collects heat, but stored water in containers or underground reservoirs and aqueducts could indeed be useful for the construction of indoor greenhouses and drinking of pure water with the aid of filters. As has been noted, the ancient Romans built an empire along with hundreds of miles of underground water reservoirs. Similarly, we have built thousands of miles of highways and railroad tracks, sometimes even tunneling through mountains.

Although there are now tunnels through mountains and extensive roads and railroads built on public land for communities instead of individuals, the means of abstracting water from the atmosphere is not yet considered acceptable as a government investment. However, most of the sun's heat absorbed by Earth is from water. Although there is more surface water in the southern hemisphere for absorbing more heat when it is now both closer to and tilted towards the sun during summer, it is gradually reversing to the northern hemisphere. Because of less surface water, less overall heat by Earth will be absorbed, but the northern hemisphere still should become warmer in the summer and colder in the winter. With the addition of greenhouse gases, the overall atmosphere should become more humid in the summer from more rain and snow during the winter, but arid climates could also become even more arid from summer heat. It would thus be wise to invest in the future for a more livable environment.

NASA has been experimenting on closed systems for future space travel. Laser light can be used to extract hydrogen and oxygen from other materials for the use of fuel with water and air being maintained as byproducts. Such experiments could also be extended to the science of climatology regarding more advanced underground aqueducts and reservoirs.

The joint effort to combat climate change includes cities, states and nations worldwide. However, even though some cities have offered such incentives as water and electric utilities purchasing electricity from home owners who generate it with solar panels, the utilities can only buy as much electricity that they can sell to maintain their services, as to either raise rates to other customers or other services. A more effective remedy could be for them to contract with home owners for permission to place solar panels on the properties to then share the profits of selling the produced electricity for more production of goods and services, but such a practice could be too politically controversial for its employment if it interferes with other commercial production of products.

The goal is also to aid the innovation of free enterprise instead of disrupting it. Some states have taxed the use of carbon fuel with the incentive of credits for the manufactures to invest in alternative energies. Still, job security of coal mining and oil drilling is threatened. However, since oil drillers produce about seven times more water than they do oil and natural gas, a small amount of excess water from oil drilling has been used for de-icing roads, dust prevention, and combating forest fires that have continually been increasing from more electric storms and stronger winds. A small portion of the water is also flow-back water used to help the drilling process. Some of the water is radioactive and more saline than ocean water, but with the aid of new scientific technology and more extensive purification by bio-char it could be purified for both drinking and more extensive agricultural use.

Forestation instead of deforestation is critical to combating climate change, as plant life absorbs the carbon dioxide from the atmosphere for the benefit of animal life. Greenhouses for growing food could be beneficial on arid and semi-arid lands if water becomes economically available. Abstracting it from the atmosphere chemically, or from the use of alcohol fuels is expensive. Even the use of pure hydrogen as a fuel is dangerous and a threat to the upper ozone layer protecting us from too much ultraviolet light. More viable would be scientific projects using the produced water from oil companies. By government grants financed by such means as selling bonds to the public for it to share in the profit (as perhaps for retirement income and medical insurance), water could be purchased from oil companies and purified. It need not only profit the oil companies along with the public and stock owners being partly oil company owners, it could combat the corruption of growing opium and other drugs as well. By contracting with other countries, freeing victims of corruption could be offered to be participants of an experimental development of a greenhouse development of arid lands that are otherwise unlivable to most of us. Moreover, although the development could compete with present production of product, the production by the otherwise poor could possibly increase demand for both the consumption and production of more overall wealth.

Such a project could be carried out on several levels. On a state level, the semi-arid land in the eastern parts of Washington, Oregon and California could be developed. On a global level, the World Bank of the United Nations could contract with countries of the Sahara Desert, Mexico, Afghanistan and so forth for the prospect of both more peaceful conditions and prosperity at large.

As of now, the conditions of Climate Change by the use of carbon fuel needs to be in a way it does not pollute the atmosphere. Even the use of combining oxygen and hydrogen as a fuel with its byproduct being water can be harmful by depleting the upper ozone layer of heavy oxygen that protects us from too much energetic ultraviolet radiation of sunlight to cause skin cancer instead of only creating vitamin D for human health. In this respect, there is also a nitrogen cycle to consider. Air contains by weight more nitrogen than oxygen. It stabilizes the energy of oxygen in the atmosphere, but it is only useful as fertilizer for plant life if converted by worms, bacteria or scientific method in combining the nitrogen with hydrogen, as in the form of ammonia, $NH_3$.

Water is the key element for conditional balance. Although the consumption of carbon is needed to fuel animal life, water is needed to grow the plant life for suitable carbon consumption. Although too much water is also hazardous in flooding and the destruction of property and life, much more water is still needed for the growth of plant life. The greater amount of water simply needs to be contained with more favorable conditions. In this sense, the term 'beaver-engineering' is applicable.

Beavers create aqueducts and reservoirs for storing more water instead of allowing more of it to flow back to the ocean.

Water is both essential and hazardous to life. We tend to populate nearer to rivers and lakes contrary to arid and semi-arid environments. Flooding does result in the destruction of property and loss of life. Although there have been attempts to control the weather, as by filling the atmosphere with chemicals to cause more rain, flooding from one hurricane can supply enough water to fill billions of swimming pools. Simply put, the atmosphere is too large for us to directly control its natural effects. On the other hand, massive 'beaver-engineering' by countless different methods is both a secondary and productive means of controlling the water supply to reverse global warming.

Beaver-engineering has a successful history. As already mentioned, the Romans built a huge empire along with an elaborate structure of miles and miles of mostly underground aqueducts and reservoirs. The construction of the Grand Coulee dam in the state of Washington provides electricity along with a prosperous farming community. Countless dams and reservoirs are likewise beneficial here and there. Extracting water from more humid air to allow more natural flow along with water usage in arid regions could also be beneficial.

More beaver engineering could indeed be beneficial. Dust from the Sahara Desert of Africa reaching Florida since the 1970s has attributed to the destruction of coral reefs. The Sahara Desert is more than three thousand miles from near the Red Sea to near the Atlantic Ocean. It is the most arid region of Earth's surface, but there are underground flows of water from the Atlas Mountains and other mountainous areas that provide flourishing oasis here and there.

The main population of Egypt has flourished beside the Nile River, but the Nile Valley could become flooded by the rise of sea levels from global warming. Storing water in the part of the Sahara Desert in Egypt, similar to the Roman aqueducts and reservoirs, could be an effective counter. Moreover, although the desert is hot and dry, sunlight and trade winds blowing southwest towards the equator are plentiful for the developmental use of solar energy that could be used to tunnel into the desert whereby water could be collected, transported and stored with more efficiency with productive use, as for underground-greenhouse-gardens protected from the sandy wind of the desert. Sturdy dome structures atop the soil could also counter the destructiveness of the wind, as by slowing it down and causing it to flow higher.

Algeria, with its populated area bordering the Mediterranean Sea, has invested in solar energy of sunlight and wind. It also supplies Europe with a large amount of natural gas. Although the natural gas can pollute the atmosphere with too much hydrogen, it would not be a pollutant if used in a confined manner, as underground or within a sturdy enough structure. If controlled with underground use, the hydrogen and carbon of the natural gas, $H_4C$, combined with nitrogen and oxygen of the air could be converted to water and a fertilized form of nitrogen for plant growth. The plant growth, in turn, would resupply the atmosphere with oxygen and nitrogen. Moreover, although excess hydrogen in the atmosphere can contribute to global warming, as water absorbing heat, hydrogen can also be converted to helium, which is already done for commercial purposes. The helium could then be used for solar powered blimps to transport water to desert greenhouses and also transport products from those greenhouses to wherever needed, slowing down the wind in the process.

Such investments in the future could pay for themselves in the present. Economic wealth is essentially product; money is merely a means of credit to facilitate such investment. More food, water and livable environment could result in a fair distribution of wealth for the promotion of peace and prosperity. In Afghanistan, as previously noted, farmers have taken to grow opium because of it being able to grow in the arid climate that nutritional crops are now unable to do. More future drought will result in economic revolt for the need of survival.

The investment could be shared, as in analogy to a stock exchange, whereby the elderly could receive a retirement income. If there are fewer products in the future, then inflation reduces retirement income whereby our grandchildren become more in debt instead of having products aplenty to spend their money on. Prosperity is thus achieved by investing in the future, whether by free enterprise or by government. The latter could be more effective for environmental concern in the sense water along with air is essential to life but too plentiful for economic value, as to be an economic burden to industrial pollution. Politically, there is the need to overcome "me first" to the extent it decreases social wealth for the overall population.

In nature, there already exists cycles of change. In the far western continental states, for instance, there is about a twenty-year cycle between drought and more rain. An extreme rainy period occurs in between the drought years. Such cycles that now occur are not new; what is new is the increase to the extreme for more severe effects. Along with successive drought and extreme flooding are more frequent and more severe hurricanes and tornadoes, melting of glaciers, rising sea levels, ocean acidity, dust storms, more spread of such diseases associated with malaria fever and salmonella outbreaks, and a decrease in both marine and animal life, including more human deaths because of starvation and other effects due to climate change.

These results are now the carbon footprint of the atmosphere from our excessive use of hydrocarbon fuels. There is more usable energy in the atmosphere, but it is more uncontrollable, as evident of the increase in more natural disasters related to climate change. To counter this change, we can build sturdier structures to withstand it, pollute less, and clean up the mess we create, and we could find ways to control and use the atmospheric energy in less harmful ways.

The energy in the atmosphere can also be tapped. Besides wind and photoelectric cells for mechanical and electrical power, carbon and water can be recycled for commercial use, as they are vital parts of the food chain. Carbon itself is naturally produced in countless forms. It can be crystalline in the form of diamonds and graphite. Diamonds are more of an insulator of heat and electricity; graphite is ideal for conducting heat and electricity and can be used as an electrode. Russia, China, Turkey, India, Madagascar, Canada and Mexico are the main nations producing graphite, but it is now more commercially produced by heating the coke of petroleum by means of electricity. Such granite as charcoal can be produced effectively by heating such vegetarian waste as wood with enough heat and time in a container separating it from oxygen, which would result in combustion and polluting the atmosphere with carbon dioxide.

If we filled the atmosphere with giant blimps, as unmanned computerized drones electrically powered by sunlight and wind, they could use the atmospheric energy for more productive use instead of more hazardous effects. For instance, they could extract water and carbon from the atmosphere and transport it to where it is needed for agriculture and so forth. It would take an enormous number of blimps to reverse global warming, but the effort could be rewarding both economically and environmentally. If located most efficiently, as to be able to extract water from areas of greater humidity, as is the equator. By using the natural directions of the winds, the atmosphere could become controlled by commercial use instead of it remaining uncontrollable. Moreover, enough giant blimps in the sky might provide a superhighway for the travel above water for not increasing the sea level, and for a network of fishing, gaming and whatever.

Blimps are not a total solution to climate change, but they could still be part of the solution.

Other remedies could entail better use of material resources. As glaciers continue to melt, rising sea levels could be prevented by building reservoirs to hold more water. The downstream flow of fresh water from the mountains to the oceans could be slowed for more useful applications of it. Reservoirs along with storm forecasts could also regulate the flow of water in preventing flooding from too rapid change in the weather, as in too much early melting of winter snow.

At NASA there has been scientific effort to perfect a natural carbon cycle for future travel in space. As hydrocarbons, air and water are consumed to convert into $CO_2$ and methane gas of carbon and hydrogen convert to $CH_4$. Indicated as the most efficient means of recycling the $CO_2$ and $CH_4$ back to air and water is the use of different light frequencies of laser light.

Here on Earth, the scientific conversion can be combined with solar and other natural resources. Solar wind and light can be used to separate water into hydrogen and oxygen. The hydrogen alone can be used as fuel with air to create energy with a byproduct of water. Computerized blimps, as giant drones, can transport the hydrogen from the equator while decreasing the potential magnitude of hurricanes with the use of wind power along with sunlight energy. (Although the hydrogen can be explosive, it explodes mainly up instead of down because of it being the lightest of all the elements.)

The means of accomplishment are available. They just need to be technically understood in the manner of beaver engineering. Beavers create dams and deeper reservoirs to maintain greater water supply. The climate change solution is similar; it is just a lot more technical and complex. It is more technical in the sense more scientific study is needed to determine the impact of feasible solutions and how they can be efficiently implemented. It is more complex in the sense different areas of impact are conditional to the nature of their terrains. Blimps following the Atlantic winds from the equator into the Gulf of Mexico can more easily serve the deserts of Mexico. Water can more easily be preserved in the states of California, Oregon and Washington during increased rainfall. Deeper reservoirs might again be created in the mountains of California. Excess snow and water in the Cascades of Oregon could be diverted to fill the countless wells that already exist east of the Cascades, as underground water has been detected by colored water to flow all the way to New Mexico. Alcohol or hydrogen-oxygen fuel can be substituted for gasoline for water as a byproduct. Excess water from the Great Lakes could be channeled all the way to Arizona and New Mexico. These measures might even be needed in order to prevent future flooding conditions for a safer future.

The remedies might seem expensive, but a review of economic history indicates the cost is more feasible than it might seem, and that the investment can result in greater economic prosperity of the present as well as the future.

## 4

## RISE OF CIVILIZATION

The early rise of civilization is relevant insofar as it involves unity and conflict of people adapting to new forces of nature. It was influenced by a declining ice age from which sea levels about eleven thousand years ago were about three hundred feet lower than present levels today. Floods followed along with the development of agriculture and larger communities of people.

As other animals compete to survive hazardous threats of life, as from other animals or environmental conditions, we humans also have a tendency to deceive, steal and kill for enhancing our lives, but as some other animals also do, we unite together in order to survive more overbearing hazards confronting us. For instance, flooding plains became another challenge to survive, as to influence how we joined together to overcome hazardous elements of nature in allowing us more freedom to develop our individual efforts to gain in economic prosperity. Farming thus became a prosperous way of life. However, we humans are also inclined to become ruthless warriors, as to compete against ourselves in order to survive and prosper even more. Hunting behaviors of cavemen thus remain part of our competitive behavior as well. We kill for sport in similar manner dogs are inclined to bark because of their instinct to use their vocal chords.

It is evident we have evolved from pre-humans, which is prehistory in the sense established history is documented by writing, as was preserved on stone tablets. Nonetheless, there is still a lot of archaeological knowledge uncovered of our prehistory indicating how our civilization has evolved.

Such cultural aspects of individualism likely dominated in slavery and war in both prehistory and early history. There has been a gradual change with the population growth of farming communities and political economics. In the United States of America, for instance, women and colored people have eventually been allowed to vote, but equality of employment and wages is still controversial.

At the peak of the last ice age, which occurred around 18,000 BC, the climate was generally cooler in the northern hemisphere. The warming that followed was gradual, but it brought about more rainfall along with melting of glaciers. Some valleys were either permanently flooded or frequently flooded. The Mesopotamian Valley north of the Persian Gulf, for instance, was not inhabitable on a permanent basis until about 5000 BC, even though agricultural settlements were established in the southern part of Asia before 8000 BC.

There was extensive development here and there. The oldest known grave site dates back to about 7000 BC at a location that is now Latvia bordering the Baltic Sea along with Sweden. Settlements also occurred about 7000 BC in the Zagros Mountains, where what is now southwestern Iran. Another ancient settlement about this time was Jericho located north of the Dead Sea (Sea of Salt), which borders between eastern Jordan and western Israel, and it is now about eight hundred feet below sea level.

Although no grave site has been found as evidence of a first permanent settlement at Jericho, there was a massive wall twelve feet high surrounding it, as for protection against flooding and/or against an invasion from other people. The initial settlement lasted a few centuries before being invaded by people who ruled over the people of the initial settlement. Succeeding settlements declined as well. About twenty new settlements occurred.

Another site, Catal Huyuk, was located where what is now the western part of Turkey. Various sites of farming communities date farther back, as to about 8000 BC. They were located in the foothills of northern Mesopotamia beside the Zagros Mountains of Iran.

Archaeologists of India have claimed evidence of an early civilization having existed in the Indus Valley of where what is now parts of northwestern India, Pakistan and Afghanistan. Sonar scanning has detected large scale structures, and the wood has been carbon dated farther back than the seventh millennium BC. The archaeologists also claim it is evident a civilization of people once existed about 7500 BC along the Gulf of Cambay, which is an inlet of the Arabian Sea at the west coast of India.

The origin and destiny of these people are not established, but the civilization is believed to have been a victim of catastrophic flooding, and there is one theory proposing that some of the people survived as the origin of Sumerians in Southern Mesopotamia.

The origin of the Sumerians is also not established. A likely candidate, as proposed by Ashok Malhotra and other historians, is that they migrated from the Indus Valley. Evidence is claimed in that there appears to be similarities of skeletons of ancient tribes in the Indus Valley whereby ancient people living farther southeast nearer to Australia and having a language similar to ancient Sumerian could have migrated to Sumer. Although the evidence for this theory is not proven, as the original language of these earlier people is erased by centuries of dominant development of other languages in its place, the Sumerian literature did contain tales of catastrophic flooding along with knowledge of the seas, and the Indus Valley has also been prone to flooding, as still occurs of more than twelve percent of India.

In ancient times, melting glaciers in the Himalayas resulted in a greater amount of flooding. In any case, satellite images support Vedic claims that a gigantic river once existed. Moreover, the largest civilization during its time is believed to have existed in the Indus Valley of India and Pakistan, where it is possible a southern sea people survived an enormous flood to migrate along the coastline of the Arabian Sea into the Persian Gulf towards a drier land just west of the Mesopotamian valley.

From that drier land, they eventually migrated into Sumer when it finally became inhabitable on a permanent basis about 6500 BC. They first spoke an agglutinative language containing one-syllable words combining in ways that do not lose individual meaning. They further developed writing and pioneered the growing of grains from about 5500 BC. About 4800 BC, they began developing canals for the irrigation of agriculture.

People making eloquent pottery lived in foothills east of the Tigris River and Sumer, where what is now southwestern Iran. The area was inhabited as early as 7000 BC. Such city states as called Susa had emerged about 4000 BC. According to their own language of the time, the people called themselves Haltamtu, but much later, as according to another language, they are identified as Elamites of Elam.

Elamites differed from the people of that other language, who were a later combination of Sumerians of different peoples in the southern part of Iraq. They had combined by means of Akkadians from northern Mesopotamia invading the Sumerians in the south.

There is also a possible reference to Susa as Shushan in the Hebrew Bible. It is noted that the Biblical Elam was the son of Shem and a grandson of Noah. However, Ancient names were also meaningful titles, as in contrast to surnames of today, and their origins are confusingly complex. According to the Semitic language of Akkadians, for instance, the land of Elam meant highland. Similarly, people living in the southern part of Mesopotamia that are historically known as Sumerians had also obtained their name from the Akkadians, but the name Akkad itself is of non-Akkadian origin. The Sumerians as a mixture of Ubaidians, as previous occupants of the city state Ubaid, and Akkadians of Semitic origin described themselves as having dark heads, whether just brunettes or dark skin people.

The Akkadian language, as a variant of the Semitic language, does not prevail in the same context of more modern literature. Mesopotamia itself is a Greek word Greeks had used to refer to the valley between the Euphrates and Tigris Rivers, and the name Greek itself was not originally part of the Greek language. The name Greek derives from the Latin name Graecia, as from Romans naming of a tribe of Hellenic people living in Epirus. The Greeks referred to themselves as Hellenes. History in accordance with language is thus more complex. Nonetheless, Genesis 10:10 of the bible states Nimrod as king or lord of Akkad, and hundreds of documents have been found in both the Sumerian and Akkadian languages.

Farming communities began emerging about 6500 BC in the northern region of Mesopotamia as well as its southern region. It is believed people residing in the north generally spoke some form of language of Semitic origin, possibly as part of the more general groups of such later people becoming known as Subarians, Ammorites, Akkadians, Assyrians, and Hittites.

It is also evident a culture of people called Badarians settled along the eastern shore and southern part of the Nile River about 5000 BC to live on a diet of wheat, barley, lentils, tubers, fish and animals. Pits indicate the use of granaries. Smoking of fish is also indicated as a method of preservation. Large pottery too fragile to transport further indicates permanent but small settlements. Their tools included scrappers and axes. Domestication of animals included cattle, sheep, goats and dogs. The latter are now believed to have evolved from wolves in Northeast China about 15,000 years ago, or longer. Because such wolf-like instincts were still among them as stalking of prey, they were excellent herders of sheep that bundled for self-protection. Barking dogs also warned against the intrusion of strangers.

The Badarians were not isolated. They traded with surrounding people whereby elephant ivory most likely was acquired from farther south. They also obtained copper from northern areas. However, peaceful trade is not indicative in all respects. Injuries of the people are evident from skeletons found at their grave sites, which is indicative of competitive conditions of survival, as from hazardous climate, confrontation among themselves, or confrontation with other people.

War most likely originated as a means of survival. People settled in the fertile valleys relatively had more resources to such essentials means of survival as food. They expanded their wealth by means of canals to extend the water supply to arid regions. However, with increase in population and more extreme drought, there became the have and have-nots. If those having wealth did not protect it, they were subject to conquest by other people in need. Even if not in need, conquest of other people was a competitive means of gaining control even if only of the will of determination motivated by possible fortune for the power of accomplishment.

With such advance of civilization, as had occurred during the upcoming Bronze Age, the spoils of war became more enticing. The means of war proliferated along with the advance of material wealth. If people did not share their wealth, a revolution by means of war seems more inevitable as an alternative means of survival. Those who competed against harsher conditions in order to survive were likely inclined towards a harsher nature, and leaders of the wealthy likely became ruthless to obtain their role of leadership and secure it against a coupe. People in fear of change and conquest are also more likely to support a stronger leader, no matter how ruthless.

Along with the development of nations, greater weaponry and economic wealth, competition among leaders likely escalated for the dominance of power. However, friendly trade among nations escalated as well.

An early Bronze Age began developing in the Middle East about 3300 BC, but the tin from there contained arsenic. The alloying of tin with copper thus resulted in a toxic bronze. A non-toxic tin was thus needed in order for it to smelt with copper in producing a healthier bronze alloy. The non-toxic tin came later from European areas of Spain, England, France and Portugal about 2000 BC. Evidence from sunken ships found in the Mediterranean Sea indicates a trade route existed from those areas to Egypt and Mesopotamia.

The advanced civilizations of Mesopotamia and Egypt became central to trade. The name Egypt is also not originally from Egypt; it derives from a later time of Greek mythology whereby Aegyptus was the king of Arabia and Egypt. Ancient Egypt was previously known as the land of Kemet, meaning the land of dark soil. It might have received its name because of a flooding of the river Nile over the land to fertilize it with a soil silt rich in nutrients.

Along with trade were developments of communication, government, writing and so forth. Earliest writing in Egypt was pictographic. Other writing developed independently here and there, as in China, Europe, Asia Minor, Egypt, the Indus Valley, Egypt, Crete, and southern and northern Mesopotamia. The Sumerians seem to have advanced it sooner prior to the Bronze Age. Their language was a cuneiform script. During the third millennium BC, the pictographs at Sumer developed into a symbolic script that continually became refined of less symbols with more general abstract meanings. However, they did not develop an alphabet. The first alphabet has been credited to the Phoenicians, who became very prosperous during the Bronze Age as a maritime civilization.

The Phoenicians called themselves Sidonians, as from the city known to them as Sidon. They might have also originated the name Phoenician in honor of a king named Phoenix. Another possibility is that Sidonians were called by the Greeks Phoenicians because they sold a purple dye made from oyster shells. They are associated with Canaanite peoples that inhabited the area of Lebanon, Israel, Palestine, West Jordan and southwest Syria. Canaan also had a Hurrian-Semitic meaning similar to that of the Greek meaning of Phoenicia referring to people who produced and exported purple cloth, which could have become the naming of a city selling it, and the Phoenician maritime empire of cities centered along the Mediterranean Coast near Lebanon and Syria. Phoenicians, no matter what was the origin of their name, thus became the primary instruments of trade and commerce in the Middle East by means of the seas.

The advance of civilization was classified in relation to the Bronze Age by the historian Christian Jorgensen Thomsen. As Bronze trade began in the fourth millennium BC, an early Bronze Age began in Egypt about 3150 BC along with its north-south unification about 3100 BC and the building of the Great Pyramid of Giza completed about 2560 BC. A Middle Bronze Age, as classified, is claimed to have occurred from about 2055 to 1650 BC followed by a Late Bronze Age that began in the sixteenth century BC and lasted on into the eleventh century BC.

The Bronze Age extended into Europe from such development of civilization on such Mediterranean Islands as Crete where the Bronze Age also began about 3,000 BC. Stone tools have been found on Crete dating as far back as one-hundred and thirty thousand years ago. It could indicate the use of boats, but the sea levels were much lower in the past. Modern human population dates back to about ten-thousand BC. A Minoan civilization, named after a legendary ruler Minos of the city Knossos, flourished during the Bronze Age from about thirty-five hundred to eleven hundred BC. Original script, Linear A, found on it has not been deciphered, as no similarity to a Rosetta Stone that was found containing both Egyptian and Greek script has been found, but a later Linear B script of a combination of Minoan and Greek language is evident.

Although the island was ravaged by a volcano, earthquakes and tsunamis, it flourished between 2700-1450 BC. Extensive waterways, such as aqueducts, were built along with three story buildings and palaces having running water to drink and clean. Cisterns collected water from flat roofs. Water was even treated by flowing through a porous clay pipe. Cattle, sheep, goats and pigs were some of the domesticated animals raised. Diets included grapes, figs, olives, lettuce, celery, pears and fish, and so on.

The rise of civilization brought about both prosperity and conflict. As an analogical example, consider the nature of penguins on the continent of Antarctica. In the freezing cold of their winter they are socially cooperative in bundling together. Because the penguins near center become too warm, they go outside to cool off while the rest of them close inward for more warmth, thus creating a natural cycle for preservation of the group. In their springtime, when the females lay their eggs, the males and females are also cooperative in taking turns protecting the eggs while the other mate goes to the ocean for food. However, some of the penguins cheat on their mates in causing confrontations. When the eggs hatch into young penguins, they are cared for by their parents, but when the young ones finally begin to explore on their own, they are harassed by older penguins protecting their territories to sometimes even kill the intruders.

We are also animals. Our animal nature is just more complex. We group together for protection and build walls among ourselves. We devise rules of conduct in order to live in harmony. We compete for both survival and leadership, as for both war and peace.

In early times, our leaders were priests claiming to be messengers of gods, or even being gods, in supporting customs that pleased the gods controlling such forces of the world as weather. Some priests also became astrologers in claiming to know how to predict the weather. However, the names of gods became divine in themselves. Because names differed according to language, and the customs of worship differed among different tribes, conflict was virtually inevitable for people set in their ways resisting change.

Human sacrifice became a ritual practiced on both sides of the Atlantic Ocean, and it is also typical of war. As the wealth and commerce increased among nations, the zest for power and control became more the means of this human sacrifice than the ritual itself. Ancient Mesopotamia, along with most other people of the time, believed each person had a god protector (as a guardian angel). Each city state, too, had its protector god, as supposedly there is a spiritual entity for everything and every concept. As communities became city states, favorite gods became more powerful. Assur of Assyria, for instance, who was associated with Mount Epic in being a sacred place of worship, became considered as the father of all gods and the creator of the universe, but Babylonians regarded Marduk instead as most high.

As Sumer itself evolved into city states, each having their own temple of a deity, they began warring among themselves, and then with Elamites, who thus united together as well. The trend merely escalated.

With the Babylonian conquest of Sumer (whereby an empire became religiously named in connotation to the tower of Babel) Marduk is given more than fifty titles, including the god of life and light. Similar to Enlil, who he replaced, he ruled the air as a god of thunder and lightning. He eventually became creator god of all mankind and the world.

To the Canaanites, El was a word for god whereby name and title were synonymous in meaning. Furthermore, as patriarchal god of the Canaanites, El held such titles as *El Shaddai*, meaning lord of the mountains; as *El Roc*; meaning visionary; as *El Elyon* (*Elohim*), meaning most high; and as *El Olam*, meaning eternity for everlasting life hereafter. There is thus god considered most high, a god of a mountain (as for ascension), a god of everlasting life, and so forth. Such attributes can be regarded as spiritual in their own right, which leads to opposing possibilities: 1) these attributes became titles of the polytheistic worship; or 2) they became known as gods, spirits, angels, or to whatever they served for the ultimate good of the one true God. However, to opposing nations, differing in customs, they became an excuse for war instead of a means of relating to another form of spiritual essence.

For the sake of economic wealth and its security, imperialism became a common objective. A Babylonian Empire was an early leader of this quest. Babylon was a city of the Akkadian Empire established about 2300 BC. In 1792 BC, Hammurabi became the ruler, and he established a law code mostly in the context of an eye for an eye. For instance, a man was sentenced, as an alternative to death, and as to compensate an owner of an orchard for a tree cut down without permission, one-half mina (unit of weight) of silver. If a son was killed, the father was given the right to kill a son of the man that did the original killing. If a physician failed to save the life of a slave of a freeman, the physician was required to replace the slave with another slave.

The Babylonian Empire entailed the conquest of the southern part of Mesopotamia before conquering all of it. It continued with the conquest of the Elamites, Guitians and Kassites to the east, Semitic States (Syria) to the west, and part Asia Minor (Turkey). After the death of Hammurabi, in 1750 BC, the empire crumbled due to internal conflict for power and control.

The demise of the Babylonian Empire is typified by the last king of Ur, Ibbi-sin, who succeeded his father, Shu-sin, about 1964 BC. Shu-sin had about a hundred and seventy-mile-long wall constructed between the Tigris and Euphrates Rivers. It was supposed to keep out the Assyrians who were experiencing a long drought in their land. It did not work. Ur was overpowered, which is less likely to occur today of established world powers even though arid lands are still a problem regarding such options of growing and selling opium and other unlawful drugs. Instead of building a wall between us, and having the distribution of wealth controlled by a few, a better option could be a world organization to combat drought and climate change in a way there is a feasible distribution of wealth for all of us to succeed and contribute to economic prosperity, peace and world order.

The Persian Empire ruled by Cyrus the Great dominated about 550 BC. It originated in the northern part of Iran and extended to the southern part of Iran, into Anatolia (Turkey), Egypt, northern India and central Asia. It weakened with its attempt to conquer what is now Greece, which later became dominate under the rule of Alexander the Great.

Later empires of significance were the Roman, Napoleonic and British. A later failure was the attempt of Adolf Hitler of Germany. The subsequent dominance of the Soviet Union and the United States of America came to a standstill with the nuclear threat of each capable of destroying the other as well as civilization on Earth as we know it.

Customs have thus been a means of preferred behavior. Some of them have originated before the beginning of civilization, which resulted in both economic innovation and wars for the control of its wealth. Later, such different systems as laissez faire economics developed in France and mercantilism developed in England. The laissez faire wealth of France was based on agriculture. The mercantile wealth of England was based on gold and the manufacturing of wealth. In the United States, there was sort of a north and south division whereby southerners depending more on agriculture were more custom to the economics of France, whereas northerners tended more towards mercantile policies for controlling wealth. There are lessons to be learned from the positives and negatives of both policies for a more prosperous future of mankind in general.

It is now evident that mankind is now its own worst enemy, such that political economics needs to evolve as a more peaceful means to cooperate amongst ourselves than by war. Although a threat of a nuclear holocaust causing the destruction of human civilization has most likely deterred the motive of war between major powers, and the threat of climate change could perhaps further provide more incentive for a common purpose that could, in turn, promote world peace, there is still a need for a fairer distribution of economic wealth. More prosperity for us all in that equality is most likely a requisite for a true world peace without revolution by means of terrorism.

# 5

# POLITICAL ECONOMIC HISTORY

# OF

# EUROPE

Helpful to improving our present economic situation is to understand how it came to be what it is. A history of economics, as from ancient times to Adam Smith, is thus reviewed in detail. Although Adam Smith is considered the founder of modern economics, substantial contributions to its development included many political economists prior to him.

Economics associates with trade, which could simply have begun from the making of Stone Age tools to trade with hunters for food, such as from obsidian in Anatolia as early as 12,000 BC. With development of agriculture as a more complex societal development, a more convenient means of barter for cattle and other commodities was grain, as more available conditions to produce it rendered it more dependable for the survival of the community. However, it required an intelligible means of record keeping. In Sumer, for instance, a token was impressed on a ball of clay, as bulla, containing other tokens inside the ball. The outer token became a seal of identity, and it further ensured that it had not been tampered with. This means of record keeping was popular up until the Bronze Age when metal became the more convenient means of exchange.

Codes of Menes, who established the first dynasty of Egypt, stated that the values of gold and silver are two and a half parts of silver for every part of gold. Coinage eventually followed, as in China where copper coins were in use from 206 BC to 220 AD by the Han Dynasty, and they have been reported to have been found in tombs that date as far back as the eleventh century BC. More to the west, gold as money was

35

used as early as 643 BC in Lydia, as where now is present day Turkey, where the smelting of gold from silver into gold produced gold coins by 560 BC. Gold subsequently became common as the most preferred means of exchange. However, it has not always been preferred. A fiat currency in the form of a tally stick was authorized by King Henry I, even for the use of paying taxes, due to a gold shortage in England around 1100. Not until 1819 was a gold standard legalized in England, and the USA dollar was not redefined until 1900 to consist of twenty-five and four-fifths grains of gold, as one and three-fifths grams, although there had been an 1873 Congressional Act in the USA legislature that had omitted defining the dollar by weight of a silver dollar.

A form of money was printed on animal skin in China during the reign of Wu Ti, as just before the birth of Christ. Its use in China increased with the invention of the printing press. The Tang Dynasty from 618 to 907 printed, around 800, what was called "flying money" that was easily lost to the wind from customers transporting goods by ships at sea. The printed cash tended to remain local, as where it could be reimbursed for coin, salt or liquor from the government.

Succeeding dynasties improved the quality of paper money for a more convenient use of it by citizens in general, and its usage in China was discovered by Marco Polo in the thirteenth century. However, paper money was not officially issued by a government in Europe until by Sweden in 1601.

As for a means of regulating money, banking had occurred in ancient Egypt and Mesopotamia with the storage of grain. The process evolved for people to be able to deposit anything from grain to a precious metal for sale or trade. However, although the grain was valued for consumption, a metal soon became favored as the preferred means of exchange. Grain spoils for one disadvantage, and its quality and taste are subjective to the preference of the consumer, whereas metal is more durable and convenient for transport here and there. In particular, the rare metal of gold with its durability and shiny attractiveness would become more favorable, as typical of supply and demand economics.

Economics as part of political policy was philosophized in early times. Plato, for instance, advocated a "Credit Theory of Money" as a unit of credit or debt. Aristotle theorized property owners need to be allowed to attend to their own business in order to produce common needs of the people. He also warned that monopolization by owners could be contrary to the common interest of the people, and that interest charged on a loan is unfair in that money itself has no real value other than as an instrument of exchange.

It is also evident early banking had acquired an unfavorable reputation. Charging interest, as usury, was forbidden by the Catholic Church and by Islam. However, exceptions occurred, as by the Knights Templar and the Jews.

Accused of usury were members of the Knights Templar. They became exempt from taxation and from most local laws. Although they were also forbidden to charge interest, or a fee for holding money to safeguard, they charged rent as a loophole of the law.

The Knights Templar originated as military protectors of nobles who were often attacked and killed while on their pilgrimage to the Holy Land of Israel. The original Knights Templar consisted of only two brothers and five other relatives of Hugues de Payens. He was able to solicit permission from King Baldwin of Jerusalem for the Order that became headquartered over what is believed to have been Solomon's Temple. As they became more and more popular, they were approved around 1129 by the Catholic Church that granted them freedom to pass through borders.

Nobles graciously donated to the Knights Templar cause, as the knights had been granted charity status among countries of Europe. They were also exempt from taxation and local laws by an order of the pope. This latter condition was influenced by Saint Bernard of Chairvaux, who was the nephew of Andre de Montbard, who became Knights Templar grandmaster from 1154 to 1156.

The Knights Templar members as a charity organization were sworn to poverty, but they still accumulated great wealth and power. Their success came from recruits donating wealth for their cause, but the Knights Templar members eventually converted from military protectors to bankers by safekeeping gold in order to minimize the risk of travel. Wealthy nobles were given receipts for their gold so that they could redeem it from other Knights Templar members who located here and there.

Although the charging of interest was a forbidden act by order of the Catholic Church, the Knights Templar members engaged in many transactions, as to collect rent instead of interest for held mortgages. However, their collection of revenue competed with that of the church. Their demise finally came in 1312 at the insistence of King Phillip of France, who confiscated their wealth in order to finance his war with England. They became outlaws in all western countries of Europe except Portugal, which historically is the most profitable country whose bulk of population was to migrate to places in the new world, as about one-half of it relocated to Brazil.

Another exception to the law forbidding usury was granted to the Jews. According to interpretation of their scripture, it was forbidden for them to charge interest to other Jews, but they could charge it to non-Jews.

Jews, as from Portugal, Spain and elsewhere, were also to become early bankers, as to fulfill a need caused by the religious restrictions that had been placed on Christians. In 1396, Jews were permitted banking practice in Florence, which did not become part of Italy until 1861.

By the bribing of Pope Martin V, in 1428, they became official bankers in 1437.

A main reason the Jews were accepted as bankers is that they had been granted less rights and were thus believed to be easier to control. They had been relegated to ghetto status whereby they could be used as a middleman. As the Germanic Stein was required as part of their surnames, as to single them out from normal citizenship, they would loan and collect for debt for the so-called European nobles, but they adapted and profited just the same to gain favor of rich merchants.

Not until the sixteenth century, when Protestantism became influential, after Martin Luther led his revolt against the Catholic Church, in contesting such assertions that God's forgiveness can be bought in order not to be hell bound, was banking officially accepted as a legitimate profession of the general population.

The economics of the time was also conditional to slavery. Expansion of colonies in the new world provided more means of obtaining economic wealth, even though competition for such wealth increased in turn along with war.

Ancient Roman grapes and olives had developed into large estates that provided a source for trade, but Rome resorted to the conquest of Egypt, Sicily and Tunisia when import of grain became less obtainable. Along with such conquest was the import of slaves, which increased agricultural yield. In this tradition, France, Spain and Portugal also developed, whereas England became more dependent on their merchants trading of manufactured products from natural resources.

Spain had led the way across the seas, but France and England became challengers to the stronghold on trade in the sixteenth century.

In England, Queen Elizabeth warned that importing more goods for gold and silver than exporting would lead to poverty of its nation while enriching the foreigners of trade. Political writers were encouraged to propagandize a policy now referred to as mercantilism. It generally included high tariffs, colonization, restricting the export of gold and silver by the colonies, and forbidding colonies to trade with the use of foreign ships. Low labor wage was also encouraged for the sake of profiting from foreign trade.

Labor itself was a primary means of obtaining economic wealth. An import of natural resources could be manufactured into finished product to be exported as trade for more gold and silver. This accumulation of gold and silver was considered ideal to compensate for an increase in the population, as for funding a military along with more industrial development.

Mercantilism was mainly about collecting gold and silver for the wealth of the nation. Requiring a large fleet for protection against pirates, its effect coincided with a vigorous competition for economic wealth among nations, which further led to more conflict and outright war between them, and also revolt from colonies opposing harsh restrictions imposed on them.

In contrast to mercantilism was an economics developed in France during the eighteenth century with agriculture as its base of wealth instead of gold. An agricultural base of wealth is reasonable in that food is essential to life. An abundance of it by means of farming fertile land had previously enabled the rise of our modern-day civilization.

Even though gold is more convenient for trade, as it is more long-lasting than food, it is still a non-essential of life. In order to survive the long journey through a desert, a canteen of water is worth more than a ton of gold. Although a means of exchange is still needed for a more general free enterprise system, it is only the acceptability of gold and silver that renders them useful for trade. Egypt once used stored grain as a means of exchange. American Indians and colonial settlers traded with the use of beaver fur, fish, corn and wampum (beads of shell) as their means of trade.

In contrast to the mercantilist was thus the Physiocrat, who advocated that income from trade needs to be circular with the production of agriculture as its base value instead of merely accumulating gold and silver to finance the state of its imperial superiority. For this circular flow of money, laissez-faire economics was proposed whereby minimal intervention of the government allows freedom of interaction between economic participants. There should thus be no tariffs, as the funding of government need only be implemented by a single tax on the income of land owners. The tax was believed to provide the owners with the incentive needed for them to produce food. This movement merely paved a way for an enterprise system freer from government intervention.

A more general form of free enterprise developed in England whereby the import of natural resources had been considered needed for a creation of manufactured goods by manual labor to export for more wealth. Because the more general form of free enterprise included all products as economic wealth apart from merely agriculture as the principle form of wealth, it became a more general form of laissez faire economics.

The transition from mercantilism to laissez faire was a step-by-step process by such contributors as John Locke, Charles Davenant, Dudley North, David Hume, David Ricardo, and Adam Smith. John Locke (1632-1704) of England agreed with a supply and demand theory of price and value, and he supported individual property rights, but he also agreed with the mercantile policy of obtaining a favorable balance of trade as a competitive means of increasing wealth. Charles Davenant (1656-1714), who published an essay on trade that seemingly understood merits of competition and consumer demand, also noted that a favorable balance of exports could finance war. On the other hand, a disagreement of the policy was offered by Dudley North (1641-1691) arguing that free trade promotes wealth for both sides in allowing a division of labor as specialization. David Hume (1711-1776) pointed out that imports of gold and silver from exports increases the money supply and inflates the price of commodities, such as to render exports more expensive for the other nations to purchase, thus preventing a restoration in balance of trade. To the contrary, a principle, which is now referred to as Comparative Advantage, was proposed, after the publication of The Wealth of Nations by Adam Smith, by David Ricardo (1772-1823) whereby free trade can benefit both sides if each nation has a more efficient means of producing the products it exports.

Bernard de Mandeville developed a poetic satire that he first published in 1705. It became known as The Fable of the Bees. Honeybees robbing the flowers of their pollen and nectar support the hive in a social manner. Their pollination is essential for plants to bear fruit, but an emotional connotation for poetic drama referred to this act as individual vice, which generated criticism along with the popularization of the theme. Vice is thus individual action resulting in economic prosperity. It is an "invisible hand" that unknowingly benefits the economy, which was a phrase Adam Smith used in the religious context of a godlike intent, as opposed to vice, to prevail of individual action.

Smith acknowledged greed could have negative effects on the general welfare of society. However, the resulting negative consequence could very well be an integral part of the nature of laissez faire economics. A particular person who smokes cigarettes along with an unhealthy diet is supportive to the employment of doctors and so forth for the distribution of wealth and a prosperous economy of ample opportunity to succeed in life. In contrast, a person who eats healthy and exercises, and rides a bicycle instead of relying on an automobile for daily travel, contributes less to the economy and more to the self with less chance of environmental pollution. With more emphasis on economic wealth, there is a general trend of merchants to welcome people having more money to spend on merchandise. Wealth becomes status. The person with the more expensive watch is viewed as a more successful individual. Having a greener lawn than the neighbors is desirable. Economic wealth thus tends to be in the eye of the beholder. However, social wealth, such as a healthier climate in which to live, can also be a result one way or another in either increasing or decreasing wealth.

James Steurat Denham (1713-1789) published a comprehensive work in 1768 defending principles of mercantilism with the title: An Inquiry into the Principles of Political Economy. It was countered by his fellow Scottish writer Adam Smith (1723-1790), who was to publish his Wealth of Nations in 1776, the same year the United States of America set forth its Declaration of Independence from England. Smith's book is considered by most economic historians as establishing the foundation of modern economics.

Smith classified economics as a political inquiry into the nature of what determines the wealth of a nation's economy to provide revenue for public service. Does this classification indicate financing government is needed to determine the wealth of its people to some extent? It could be so interpreted by some of us, but Smith further advocated the concept of an invisible hand whereby a minimum amount of government allows innovation of individuals to have positive effect on the economy as a whole. However, whatever constitutes the minimum amount of government for economic welfare is controversial. Some political economists argue government only needs to provide security, as to enforce the law of the land, and to protect its borders from invasion. Others economists advocate that government has a vital role in determining such social aspects of the economy as social security and environmental concerns.

Labor had generally been viewed, even by Adam Smith, as the means of creating wealth. For a competitive advantage, a means to minimize labor cost was preferred, whether it involved the use of such animals as an ox for plowing fields, slave labor, or taking advantage of competitive conditions of the poor seeking employment. Adam Smith further warned that corporations might take advantage of the poor by means of monopolization. Discontent is indeed evident with regard to such remedies to an unfair distribution of wealth as later proposed by Marx and Engels of their Communist Manifesto. (Supposedly, monopolies and oligopolies are prevented from occurring by government, but the use of monetary wealth can also influence government officials.)

Although labor has and still does create wealth, it is not necessary itself the controlling factor of wealth. Such energies as petroleum and electricity either help produce more product or decrease the need of manual labor. If computerized robots replace the need of human labor without additional product, then the controlling factor of wealth becomes ownership rather than labor.

Ownership is further typical of economic wealth in that owners of property have more credit by means of their property as collateral. Credit becomes money. By ownership of more money, as to lend for profit, money is a means to acquire more of it (although not without risk). The competition for wealth inspires innovation for more products. However, if one competitor of free enterprise wins out, then the free enterprise system is won over by monopolization of the money supply.

The means of monopolization was somewhat different in the past than it is now in the present. As in the past, the mercantile hording of gold or storing paper money underneath a mattress could result in deflating prices of products in increasing the economic wealth of the people with more money at hand. As in the present, inflation versus deflation is more influential on who controls the economy. Inflation, with regard to an increase in wages and profits, and with regard to a fixed rate of interest on a loan, tends to benefit the borrower with an increased wage for more easily paying back the loan, whereas deflation tends to benefit the lender. Consequently, borrowing for the purchase of a house is thus a risk with regard to deflation, bankruptcy, lower wage and an inability to pay back the loan, whereas the rich become relatively richer with lower prices for future investment. However, even though the rich tend to become richer, and the poor tend to become poorer, lenders can also become victims of deflation as well. Besides the risk of loaning with no return, less production can result in poorer living conditions of the economy as a negative in rendering a more insecure society at large, unless replaced by computerized robots.

    Balance is thus needed of economics. Money earns money, as by some risk, but economic wealth should be a measure of product instead of money. Besides, economic wealth is partly only wealth in the eye of the beholder, but too much to the extreme could render the economic system dysfunctional.

# 6

## DEMOCRATIC REPUBLIC AMERICA

An influential factor of the American Revolution from English rule was interpretations of republicanism for the formation of a government. Both Plato and Aristotle independently philosophized in ancient Greece that democracy, aristocracy and monarchy combine to form a republic. Later ideas stressed the duty to enforce the law of the land by means of liberty overcoming the corruption of government. England had become viewed corrupt, as such, by colonists. However, during the American Revolution itself, the only official means of unifying the colonies was Continental Congress that had no authority to tax or regulates trade. Payment to soldiers was thus dependent on each state to authorize its contribution. An urging for a central bank for the financing of military and other obligations of government would later be included in a newly formed constitution whereby the Republic formed was contained with a President, Court, Congress and Senate. The inclusion of the Senate was a compromise whereby a number of Congress representatives are according to the population of each state, whereas each state has the same number of representatives for the Senate.

Virtues of republicanism were recognized within the colonies in a manner that rule for and by the people were favored. Republicanism, democracy and liberalism were thus uniquely intertwined in a popular way that could have enabled Thomas Jefferson to succeed George Washington as President, as a Democratic-Republican Party, popular in name, had been founded by James Madison and Jefferson. However, the authoritative nature of the new nation as a republic remained controversial. Thomas Jefferson, Thomas Paine and Benjamin Franklin asserted representative democracy as a preferred element essential to republicanism, but John Adams and Alexander Hamilton preferred more governmental control by leaders more knowledgeable of government instead of by the common people with less understanding of it.

Contributing factors of unionism began farther back in history. In 1664, the British Navy invaded New Amsterdam, what is now New York, in applying the mercantilist policy of enriching itself at the expense of colonialism. As England declined to furnish its colonies with coinage, and it even forbid them from minting their own coins, colonists were dependent on barbaric methods to barter for commodities and services. Their exports were accepted by English merchants, but they received goods and services as trade without exchange of gold in return. A method of trade amongst themselves thus resorted to such items as tobacco and rice as money in southern colonies. Included as various forms of money for colonies more in general were animal skins, livestock and so forth, but their impermanent nature and variance in value, according to supply and demand economics, were of far less convenience than that of gold.

Dutchmen in the area of New York trading with Indians introduced, in 1627, wampum (shell beads) to New Englanders as a method of trade. Ten years later, wampum became legal tender for paying taxes in Massachusetts. However, it became illegal twenty-four years later, most likely because of it being too fragile for practicality, and its productive potential could have been too uncontrollable as well, as were amounts of gold and silver in later years.

In 1652, in violation of English law, there was an attempt to establish a mint in the Massachusetts Bay Colony in Boston. It failed mainly because of its simple design being easily counterfeited. In 1684, attempts to mint coin were further thwarted with the closure of the mint by order of the King of England, Charles II, in revoking a fifty-five-year-old charter of self-management. Colony members consisted mostly of Puritans detested by the royal order for their attempt to purify the Catholic Church, and Charles II accused them of insubordination.

Colonists were still dependent on a currency for community services. A likely candidate available to them was paper money. Paper at the time was not as durable as it is now, but it could have been a more convenient means of exchange for circumstances at hand. The Massachusetts Bay Colony thus printed, in 1690, the first paper money in North America. The practice was soon followed by other colonies. However, if the paper money was not then backed by specie of either gold or silver, it would be worthless against the purchase of commodities from Europe. The paper money thus became notes of credit with the condition they were redeemable for gold and silver. However, even though owned land could have also been considered as collateral for paper credit, the notes rapidly depreciated in value because of not enough gold and silver available for redemption.

Land banks were created in the following century for the transactions of mortgages, some of which were by government agencies. A few commercial banks briefly existed. Some of them were fraudulent; others were closed for being in violation of English law, as was one established in Philadelphia by Thomas Willing and Robert Morris.

Still, such circumstances as war created a need for paper money, as was issued by the Continental Congress of so-called Continentals between 1775 and 1779 in order to help finance the Revolutionary War of Independence from 1775 to 1783. As a means of credit, a Continental dollar equated with the Spanish dollar, but too many Continentals became issued than could be redeemed for gold and silver, and they were decreased ninety-nine percent in value by 1779. The slogan "not worth a Continental" persisted even after the colonies became victorious, whereby Continental Congress enacted in 1786 a constitutional law that forbid any state or federal chartered bank to issue paper money.

The constitution did allow the borrowing of money. For the purchase of such needs as bullets and guns, the war effort had depended on financial support from patriotic and gracious donors or lenders of gold and silver, as about $11.7 million had been mostly borrowed from Dutch bankers and the French government, and about $42 million from wealthy merchants located within the colonies.

Merchants opposing English policy aided the revolt. Robert Morris Jr. was one particular merchant in the Philadelphia Bay Colony. As part owner of a shipping and trade company, having international connections, he used it to spy on the movement of British troops. His firm helped sell the spoils of war obtained from English ships by privateers. His own navy eventually was sacrificed for the cause. In addition, he personally paid 10,000 English pounds to pay continental troops under General Washington, and then by way of "Morris Notes" of his own funds, he funded more than half the cost of bullets and other governmental expenses. However, he later invested his remaining fortune in land. He went bankrupt in 1798 after the Bank of England suspended specie payments in 1797, and he served time in debtor's prison until 1801, being freed after the passage of a bankruptcy act.

A close associate to Robert Morris was Alexander Hamilton, who was an early volunteer in the revolt against English rule. Hamilton joined a New York volunteer unit in New York, received the rank of Lieutenant, and was later elected captain. He became General Washington's top staff aide with the rank of lieutenant colonial. He requested an active role in the field of battle. Washington, with reluctance to sacrifice the communication talent of his top aide, finally consented, giving Hamilton the command of an infantry battalion from New York that forced a critical surrender of the British army at Yorktown, Virginia. President Washington, on September 11, 1789, then appointed Hamilton as the first Secretary of Treasury.

Although the colonies revolted against English rule, the merchants did not oppose the English banking system. They were practitioners of it, as in need of a system of credit whereby those with wealth could invest in those unable to create wealth because of not having enough of it at hand. Up until 1781, the local means of credit relied on such individual transactions as that of an owner of land using it as collateral to obtain a loan from an individual or company. Land owners included government as well as individuals.

To help finance the war, Philadelphia merchants had established the Bank of Pennsylvania in 1780, but it was not a real bank in the ordinary sense. It resulted in rampant inflation partly due to an issue of $240 million credit in banknotes by the Continental Congress that were to be redeemed for gold and/or silver, partly because the states chartered their own banknotes, and partly because the British counterfeited the banknotes. Such factors resulted in not enough silver or gold available for all individuals to redeem notes on demand. The states and the federal government thus remained in debt after the war. However, inflationary aspects of monetary policy were internalized, whereby banks in Europe deemed the credit rating of the colonies was higher than that of England. Robert Morris, for instance, was able to obtain a sizable loan from France to establish the Bank of North America, which he also invested in. (The vast amount of open land in the new world was also an attractive investment opportunity.)

Hamilton had proposed, in 1870, to Superintendent of Finance, Robert Morris, the need for a national bank to help finance the war. Morris agreed by submitting to Confederation Congress a request to officially charter the bank. The request was granted in 1781, as the Bank of North America. It was the first privately owned bank of the United States, and it was partly financed by selling shares to the public. Morris himself was personally a prime financier of the war and of government, and the Bank of North America was partly financed by his ability of obtaining a loan from France. However, the debt kept increasing.

In response to the Bank of Pennsylvania's failed attempt to finance the war, Morris did attempt to solidify the Bank of North America with specie. However, the bank was accused of being a monopoly. The monopolization practice of the bank was actually endorsed by its backers as necessary in order to survive during the time of war, but the wartime privilege allowed discrimination of loaning practice to whomever board members of the bank preferred to loan to. More banks became more desirable for fair play.

The first constitution of the United States was an agreement called the Articles of Confederation and Perpetual Union. It was ratified in 1781, and it forbade taxation by the federal government, which could then only borrow money from the states. Congress also lacked authority to regulate the trade of states between either themselves or with foreign countries. States of the Union thus had independent control of their own trade policies. However, when the federal government failed to obtain its needs from the states, this original constitution was replaced with a new one, ratified in 1789, whereby the Secretary of Finance, Alexander

Hamilton, founded a national banking system similar to one already existing in England.

Hamilton studied such economic theory as authored by David Ricardo (1772-1823) advocating that government has a significant role in economic development. England had used public debt for building its military empire, but that does not mean the banking system was the cause of it being such a dominant force. The greed for more gold as economic wealth was more likely the controlling factor. With the unifying aspect of government in mind, Hamilton successfully proposed to Congress that it charter a national bank similar to the Bank of England. The Bank of the United States was thus chartered in 1791 for a twenty-year period.

# 7
# BANK AMERICA

A main difference between national banks of England and the USA was only that shareholders of the USA Bank had more votes for more shares, whereas the Bank of England allowed only one vote for each shareholder. Another difference was that the US Bank Charter restricted the amount of loans offered according to the amount of gold and silver in reserve, whereas the Bank of England Charter placed no such restriction. Moreover, whereas the USA government was a shareholder with twenty percent ownership, the Bank of England, for the record, was strictly privately owned.

Critics of Hamilton have labeled him as a mercantilist, as in association with Ricardo. Adam Smith had also suggested the United States of America should remain an agrarian type society instead of attempting to become an industrial one of manufacturing products. However, Hamilton was more in tune as a businessman in realizing the critical need for a financial institution for paying of debt and financing, as he had previously organized the Bank of New York in 1784.

The accusation that Hamilton was a mercantilist is rejected by some of his supporters who claim he simply realized free enterprise also requires the protection and support of government. During his time as Secretary of the Treasury, there was a national debt of more than five million dollars and a total debt of states of about twenty-five million dollars. Hamilton realized a consolidation of the state debts into a national debt could help unify the states in support of a central government. To pay for the national debt, he thus proposed the creation of a national central bank for establishing the means for credit and investment, as financed partly by a tariff on imports, partly by taxing distilled liquor, and partly by selling bank shares to citizens and foreigners for the promotion of such infrastructure as roads for the growth of an industrial economy as well as the financing of military and government.

The selling of debt, as stock, is unique inasmuch as there is no redemption required of the sell. If the company of the stock fails, the investor suffers the loss. For it to become an attractive investment, taxation provided a means of securing it for future dividends. Investors of it would also be more inclined to support a financed institution of the people.

The proposal was a difficult sell, particularly to the southern states that were comprised by conservative members of the Republic, which included President George Washington. Thomas Jefferson, as the Secretary of State, favored the agrarian nature of wealth, feared a national bank would become an unfair monopoly in its competition with state banks, and he doubted the constitutional legality of the national bank. James Madison, a Representative of the House for Virginia, also objected to the proposed twenty-year charter of the bank as too long of a temporary operation. Nonetheless, in 1791, the bill for authorization passed both in the House and Senate, and Hamilton persuaded President Washington to sign it into law. Thus, First Bank of the United States was chartered for a period of twenty years between December 12, 1791 and March 3, 1811. It was headquartered in Philadelphia where it branched out into other major cities from New York to New Orleans.

The seed capital of the bank was set at ten million dollars, and it was financed as a stock of paper notes to be distributed among the economy as currency. The government was the major stock holder at two million dollars. It thus shared in the profits, but it had no direct control of its operations. The national bank also competed with state banks, but the government attempted to control availability of credit, and to even regulate the issue of notes by state banks for the purpose of national security.

The first few years of the charter were unstable. Initially, government scripts were sold as down payments for shares of the Bank. A competition for the scripts resulted in up-and-down periods of investments. However, the printing of notes was backed with the minting of coins, and the situation stabilized after a few years. Perhaps a gold discovery in North Carolina aided the cause. The USA Mint only reported, in 1793, that gold was being produced in the state. A large nugget found in 1799 by a young man, Conrad Reed, was used as a doorstep for three years until a jeweler revealed to the family it was gold.

Up until the national bank was established, all currency was foreign, as from a circulation of coins minted in Mexico and Europe. An official mint by Act of Congress enacted in 1792 became operational in 1793. Most coins contained a percentage of silver. A nickel, for instance, was half the silver of a dime. Some coins also contained gold for a monetary range in value from two dollars and fifty cents to twenty dollars. The official value of a one-dollar federal banknote was about three-hundred-one and one-fourth grains (two-hundred-fourteen and fifty-six one thousand grams) of silver, but both silver and gold would vary according to its supply and demand as well as supply and demand of various products.

The first twenty-year charter seemed successful for the most part, but its renewal rested on Vice President Clinton for his tie breaking vote, which was against renewal. In the following year, the USA got into a military conflict with England for two and a half years that resulted in a period of inflation. Not until 1816 did President Madison sign into law the second twenty-year charter, but its renewal in 1836 was to be vetoed by President Jackson, who favored presidential authority for unity of government, but he also regarded the Central Bank as a threat to monopolize the banking rights of the states.

By 1811, about seventy percent of the Bank stock was foreign owned, thus aiding the depletion of its specie reserves of gold and silver. Moreover, the agriculturists, mostly in the southern states, complained the Bank provided an unfair advantage in favoring the development of industry over agriculture. In turn, industrialists, located mostly in the northern states, complained the southerners had an unfair advantage with the usage of slavery. The debate would eventually result in the Civil War from 1861 to 1865.

A favorable argument for renewing the charter for a central bank was that about five million dollars in paper currency accounted for about twenty percent of the money supply in circulation. However, the bank notes issued by the National Bank were not discounted, as revenue by the federal government was obtained by such other means as taxation, whereas profit of state banks was dependent on a discount whereby redemption of notes could be anywhere from zero to one-hundred percent less than their initial value. The National Bank thus had a competitive advantage in offering full redemption of all its notes, which became representative of a currency of constant value. After the failure to renew the National Bank Charter, the number of state banks increased considerably from only seven-hundred and twelve.

After the war of 1812, industrialists in northern states began lobbying for tariffs on imports, which partly neutralized the wealth obtained of southern states from the export of such agricultural products as cotton that were produced by means of slave labor. The tariffs rendered imports as relatively more expensive for the benefit of financing the federal government, as for the purpose of industrial investment. When President John Quincy Adams signed the Tariff of 1828 into law, the state of South Carolina threatened to secede from the Union. President Andrew Jackson, who was inaugurated in 1829, was a Jeffersonian in favor of such state freedoms as banking, but he also considered a strong Union as beneficial to the security of its people. He thus countered the South Carolina rebellion with a show of military force. A compromise was reached whereby the duty fee on Tariffs was lowered.

Still favoring Free State banking, Jackson vetoed in 1832 the renewal of the National Bank charter due in 1836. He further used an executive order in 1833 to not fund the National Bank, and he used yet another executive order in 1836 that required the purchase of government land be paid only by either gold or silver coins. Jackson, who owned hundreds of slaves, was a recognized hero of the war of 1812, and he favored unity of states without monopolization of federal government. He helped form a Democratic party whereby its members became referred to as Jacksonian democrats.

In 1935, for the first and only time in USA history, the national debt was completely paid off. The USA economy had been prospering when Jackson became President, mainly due to export from farming, tariffs and the sale of public lands obtained from territorial expansion. Exports further provided an abundance of silver from China and Mexico. However, such a means of prosperity resulted in an inflation bubble, and the Panic of 1937 occurred along with about a seven-year recession.

The main cause of economic recession is inflation factors reversed by deflation factors. As products lower in price, those in debt become more in debt. One factor of deflation was a sharp decline of England's gold reserve due to more imports than exports, possibly due to less harvest of its wheat.

A counter to the effect of deflation was raising the interest rate to discourage borrowing in decreasing money circulation for less import purchase, depending on what consumers prefer to purchase. In this sense, a raise in interest rate is a natural result of supply and demand economics whereby less money in circulation tends to increase the need for credit, and to increase its rate as costlier. Although the people still needed such food as wheat, other imports less critical to survival would decline.

Nowadays the Federal interest rate is lowered to increase credit and money supply in circulation during periods of recession. However, banks are less willing to loan, partly because of there being more risk of default, and probably not because they can lose out to eventual inflation with their long-term loans at lower interest with more future demand to borrow it.

The USA recession related to England's change in economic policy. The yield of cotton export declined. Moreover, USA banks had relied on English Bank loans to fund such projects as industrial expansion to the west. With a stiffer price of these loans, and with gold and silver as a stiffer requirement for the purchase of government land, the result was also less loans and less competition for the purchase of land, resulting in deflation of prices as well as bank failures, less production and higher unemployment.

After a couple years or more, a recovery from the recession began. Part of this recovery can be attributed to the liberal banking policy that had been initiated by Jackson, whereby a free banking period was in effect from 1837 to 1862. During this period, state-chartered banks without the oversight of federal regulation. Although banks were required to issue bank notes in lieu of silver and gold coins, the reserve requirements and the interest rates for loans and deposits were determined according to particular state policies. A Michigan Act of 1837, for instance, allowed banks an automatic chartering with no need of consent from state legislature. As other states, in general, adopted similar policy, loans became more liberal along with bank failures, as about one-half of them within five years occurred, mostly because of their inability to redeem their notes.

Gold was also discovered in the hills of California in 1848, which was unlike the previous one in North Carolina in 1798 in that the California one attracted a large increase in population of immigrants mostly from Asia and South America, as with more than twenty-five thousand from China alone. However, very few prospectors became rich. The gold itself became an inflationary factor, which a population increase could counter, but business capitalized more by taking advantage of the increased population in catering to it in becoming a surer means of obtaining economic wealth.

Some economic analysts suggest too lenient restrictions of state banks attributed to their failures; other analysts, such as Daniel Sanches, have correlated the bank failures to an inadequate restriction of free banking whereby smaller banks were at a disadvantage. To charter a bank, states generally required a condition of collateral for notes of credit to be backed by specie or such securities as government bonds to refund the notes on demand. However, the actual value of the state bonds was subject to the stock market, which differed from their required purchase price that maintained intact as their collateral requirement. When market value of bonds lowered, and runs on banks occurred to redeem notes for specie, smaller banks tended not to have the collateral they needed to comply.

# 8
# SLAVERY CONTROVERSY AND CIVIL WAR

An influential factor in the development of Colonial America was the mercantile policy of Europe along with slavery. As European nations competed for natural resources to develop and trade for monetary wealth, as by exporting finished products for gold and silver, they resorted to low wage labor that trickled down to slavery. English law forbade the enslaving of Christians. Native American Indians were not easily controlled, and initially they were exported to be sold as commodities. Later, slaves were imported from Africa by way of Spain, France and Portugal for agrarian and mining production. Indentured servants, indentured for reimbursing their cost of transport to the new world, were another option. After serving their time, they could become free to acquire land and so forth. Even some Africans became free citizens after they were baptized. However, stringent rules along with high taxes that England imposed on its colonies contributed to revolts. A contributing factor for unification instead of revolt would be a central banking system.

John Locke (1632-1704) is considered by some historians as the founder of Classical Liberalism. He also invested in a Royal African Company for the trade of slaves and drafted Constitutions for Carolina in establishing a feudal aristocracy allowing slave owners full mastery over their slaves. He believed atheism should not be tolerated. At the time, only slavery of other Christians was outlawed. His opposing aristocracy and slavery in his writings must thus have referred to the elite, who in some circumstances are obligated to revolt against corruption. He also believed government should be divided into separate authorities.

South Carolina became the main advocate of slavery. Although it was legal in all thirteen colonies in 1776, all states except South Carolina outlawed the importation of slaves in 1808. However, the invention of the cotton gin was instrumental in providing a lucrative cotton export from plantation owners in the South with the use of slave labor. The North countered with Tariffs. Whereas the South favored independence of the states, the North favored economic unity by means of a central banking system.

Southerners obtained wealth in agriculture by means of slave labor, but manufacturing of product was the main objective of northerners. Slaves gave the South an advantage. The counters for the North were government tariffs imposed on imports, as much as sixty-two percent in 1828, resulting in relatively more expensive exports from counter tariffs from other nations. The North favored more expensive tariffs; the South favored free trade. Southern Democrats were more persuasive for a gradual lowering of the price, but conflict maintained regarding slavery itself. After the USA gained control over northern Mexico and California in 1848, the South aimed at expanding slavery into the newly controlled lands of the USA, and there was some contention of expanding its control to Cuba and into Central America.

This expansion was perceived as a disadvantage to the North. Compromise of an equal number of Slave States to Free States had previously been in effect from 1803 to 1854, but Free States had begun to outnumber Slave States. Southerners, considering this outnumbering as a threat to their practice of slavery, decided to declare their independence from the Union.

As it were, authority of government was a controversial issue with regard to state rights versus federal rights as well as individual rights versus federal rights. Some merchants felt the need of a central bank for a stronger union; others feared the central bank could become a monopoly with an unfair advantage in competing against state-chartered banks. Moreover, there was the controversy over whether states should have their own right to own, buy and sell slaves from which there was to be a civil war.

The Civil War began in 1861, and it ended in 1865 with a military victory of the North over the South for the abolition of slavery. However, neither the North nor the South had been financially prepared for war. The South typified a farming community whereas the North was inclined to specialize in banking, manufacturing and such transportation as shipping.

In order to finance the war, a source of revenue was required. A domestic tax on citizens and local products was unpopular in both the North and the South, but the North did favor an import tax, as was the main source of government revenue in the nineteenth century, and northerners were inclined to welcome it as protection of their livelihood from less expensive imports of cheaper labor abroad.

Although the cheap labor of slaves receiving only food and shelter existed in the South, the South was vulnerable to the shipping control of the North. When the South rebelled, the North responded with a blockade of southern exports, which delivered a tactical blow to the South regarding its lucrative source of southern revenue as export trade.

The tactic favored the north even though southern exports were interconnected with northern businesses as well as with European commerce. European manufacturing was able to obtain its import needs from Egypt, India and Brazil for no need to become involved in an internal conflict with the American states. Although northern states had also been affected, as they benefited from the shipping of the southern exports, and even though northern banks held bonds as their securities that had been purchased by southern states, a shortage of wheat in England further gave northern investors an alternative, which was to invest in railroads of the Midwest for the transport of wheat and other commodities.

Economic circumstances thus favored the North. However, the initial conditions still were critically challenging.

At the beginning of the war, the north was direly in need of finance in order to pay its soldiers, purchase ammunition, and so on. The interest rate from state-chartered banks ranged from about twenty-four to thirty-six percent, which did not appear affordable at the time according to certain government officials. A reconstruction of the banking system was thus sought for the purpose of financing the war, such as a security matter for the Union to prevail against opposition to its existence.

The financial situation of government, as to its lack of funding, seems contrary to the economics of the time. The free banking period from 1837 to 1862 had experienced growing pains, but it was structurally coherent for the issue of credit for the general public. There was cheating, such as counterfeiting and so forth, and booms and busts periods occurred from time to time for various reasons, such that some of the people suffered while other people were able to take advantage of the situation, but the system was feasible with the ability of the people to overcome such diversity with enough successful practice of accounting for their own individual concerns, even if adverse to national security.

During the free banking period, state-chartered banks were allowed by anyone meeting the requirements of the state charter. A strict requirement was a financial reserve to ensure bank notes could be redeemed for silver or gold on demand. A penalty was accessed for failure of this requirement, but liability deposits for the issue of notes could include government bonds that were issued either by a state or the Federal Government. As long as they remained operational, they provided a reliable source of collateral as long as the government itself did not become bankrupt, which the Union nearly did in 1860. The success of both government and banking was thus still interdependent even during the free banking era.

The reason for this lack of government funding was another situation in itself. The California gold rush in the late 1840s had helped enable prosperity in the 1850s that included a construction of twenty thousand miles of railroad tract by sales of stocks, government bonds and land grants, whereby the USA Government even obtained a surplus. Lower tariff duties were thus enacted in 1857. However, a Panic of 1857 followed a moderate recession to the economic boom. Part of this panic is attributable to the embezzlement of a branch of an Ohio Life Insurance and Trust Company in New York City. It did not help that, in September, thirty thousand pounds of gold was sunk at sea by means of a hurricane. In response to the panic, President Buchanan, with the hint that he might have to persuade Congress to pass a forfeit law to cancel any bank charter that suspended its specie payments, suggested to the bankers they hold one dollar in specie as security for every three dollars issued as paper credit. In compliance with his suggestion, credit did tighten, as to result in reversing inflation to deflation. Foreclosures and bankruptcies of such companies as railroads and even banks soon occurred along with an increase in unemployment. Tax revenue, either tariff or domestic, was thus reduced.

Such events of the recession hardly affected the southern states, as to render them a relatively enhanced means of bargaining. President Buchanan being a Pennsylvanian Democrat was inclined to compromise with the issue concerning tariffs, as to appease both northern merchants and his southern Democrats. USA tariffs, which were lowered in 1857, had become lower than most every other competing country. A fellow Pennsylvanian, Justin Smith Morrill, organized the Morrill Tariff of 1861 that Buchanan signed into law on March 2, 1861 just before Lincoln took office. Seven southern states had already succeeded from the union, and they elected Jefferson Davis president of the Confederacy.

When Abraham Lincoln was elected president November 6, 1860 as a member of the new Republican Party opposing slavery, South Carolina led the seven southern states declaring their succession from the Union. President Buchanan and President-elect Lincoln both declared the succession illegal. Lincoln, who was a member of a newly formed Republican party that had replaced the Whig party, opposed slavery and favored tariffs. After he was inaugurated President on March 4, 1861, South Carolina forced the Union army to vacate Fort Sumter in that state on April 12, 1861.

When Lincoln took office, the USA Treasury had less than one-half million dollars in specie, and it was millions of dollars in debt. Financing for the Civil War was a difficult challenge. At that time, the constitutional law stipulated Federal Government could only receive coin from banks or individuals, and banks that were only willing to make loans to the government by charging it between twenty-four to thirty-six percent interest rates. Rather than choose from more than a thousand of different bank notes of countless banks charging such high interest, the USA Government of the North chose to finance the war against the Confederate South by resorting to taxes on imports, income, property and so forth. Still, however, taxes in themselves were not an immediate solution, as lack of specie required some form of credit to pay daily expenses at a future date.

Acts by Congress permitted the government to both sell Government Bonds bearing interest, and to issue Demand Notes redeemable in specie on demand that did not bear interest. However, Demand Notes were a difficult sell, and banks only purchased them at a discount, and then loaned them to the public for additional interest. Moreover, a decrease in gold specie of both bank and government reserves occurred due to such factors as hoarding specie by the public. Moreover, the Stock Market of American Securities was, in part, held by foreign investors draining specie from it. After December 31, 1861, both banks and the government of the Union terminated their redeeming of specie.

As a means to pay the salaries of soldiers and other military expenses, Colonel Dick Taylor suggested to President Lincoln that patriotic soldiers would accept paper notes of credit not backed by specie on immediate request. On the following February, Congress authorized, by a Legal Tender Act, an issue of one-hundred-fifty million dollars in Legal Tender Notes for the replacement of the previous Demand Notes. These new greenbacks, known for green ink printed on their backsides, were legal tender, as fiat money, except that holders of the notes could not use them for paying import duties, and the government could not use them to pay interest on its bonds. They were issued as a temporary wartime measure with the assumption that specie obtained by customs duties would eventually become available to buy them out of circulation. The legal tender notes were also similar to interest paying bonds. Because the treasury did not have enough specie to redeem Demand Notes, the USA Treasury was authorized by the Legal Tender Act to pay up to twenty percent interest for the redemption of the Legal Tender Notes at a later date.

Rather than flood the economy with fiat currency, the Legal Tender Notes, known as greenbacks, were helpful in allowing citizens to use them for purchasing bonds. Secretary of the Treasury, Salmon P. Chase, hired Jay Cooke, a private owner of a banking house of the name Jay Cooke & Company in Philadelphia, to sell bonds, whose total worth was five-hundred million dollars, from October 1962 to January of 1964. Cooke was paid one tenth of five percent for the first ten million dollars' worth of bonds sold, and was paid one tenth of three eighth percent thereafter. With the use of newspapers for advertising, citizens were persuaded that it was a patriotic duty to support their government. A low cost of bonds relative to the affordability of buyers had also affected the sale, as providing the public with more opportunity to invest in the government for six percent return of interest payable in gold after five years with full maturity of bond value in twenty years. The campaign was paid for as part of Cooke's commission, and it exceeded the five-hundred million dollars by eleven million, which became immediately authorized by Congress.

Later, in 1865, Cook was again authorized to sell seven-thirty notes. He sold over three-hundred million dollars' worth of them that enabled the government to supply union soldiers and pay them their due wages. After the war, he participated in the establishment of a national banking system in helping establishing national banks at Washington D.C. and at Philadelphia. Still later, in 1870, his firm financed the construction of the Northern Pacific Railway.

Further remedies were needed to stabilize monetary supply. National Bank Acts were enacted in 1863 and 1864 with the intent to establish a national banking system of national banks with a Comptroller of the Currency as part of the USA Treasury. In 1865, non-national banks were required to pay a ten percent tax on their notes, as to withdraw them out of circulation in favor of a national currency. There was also an attempt to buy back the green backs with gold, but in being popularly declared "good as gold", they became preferable as the common means of circulation.

Although a national banking system was established similar to modern times, a particularly notable aspect critical to winning the war was bypassing banks in selling affordable bonds directly to the public in providing it with the opportunity to directly invest in its government. Especially essential to the potential of this investment is a government source of revenue. During and soon after Civil War times, the essential source of revenue equated to a tax and security of funding in relation to specie, which differs from modern times whereby specie has been replaced with fiat currency. This fiat money of today is worth only what it can purchase. If there is product aplenty for a dollar, then a dollar is worth an aplenty amount of product. Money thus becomes useful as a convenient means of exchange of various products, and as credit for a means of investment allowed by a money supply for more opportunistic means of creating economic wealth. Therefore, economic wealth becomes dependent on the allocation of public debt instead of the taxation of specie as collateral in itself valued as a product of labor and its demand.

# 9

# CHANGE AND ADJUSTMENT ECONOMICS

Proponents of a gold standard argue it limits inflation inasmuch as the gold supply is relatively more constant compared to an unlimited amount of paper money that can more easily be printed. Although gold rushes have inflated economies, the periods of inflation have been relatively short and mild to allow natural adjustment by members of society affected by it. However, a gold standard counterargument is that there can be a lack of gold in circulation, either of gold coins or paper credit secured by a gold reserve, which can benefit the rich by them hoarding it. By decreasing the distribution of monetary capital in circulation, it allows deflation to result from supply and demand economics whereby the same gold purchases more of the same product due to the product selling at lower prices. Those of us poor in debt with high interest loans become losers if increase in cost of interest and loss of income is greater than the decrease in cost of product.

Banking policy itself, with or without a gold standard in place, can further be at odds with total economic adjustment. Inelastic currency after the Civil War, for instance, resulted in such problems as unfavorable circumstances for farmers to finance their planting and harvesting of crops. At planting time, farmers needed loans in order to purchase seed and equipment. After harvesting and selling their crops, farmers tended to deposit much of their profits in member banks of the national banking system. The money supply of national banks thus fluctuated. The reserve requirement restricting how much banks can loan required banks to either sell bonds or stocks, or call in loans. Without enough credit to plant and harvest, farmers became bankrupt in surrendering their mortgages to banks. Financial crises occurred in 1873, 1884, 1893, and 1907, the latter being the worst in the USA before the Great Depression of the 1930s.

In the latter half of the nineteenth century, developed nations tended to comply with a gold standard as a common currency for a simpler means of comparing the values of other local currencies between nations. In 1873, the USA followed this trend in redefining the dollar in terms of gold instead of silver, and it adopted the gold standard outright in 1900. The crises of 1907 further led to the creation of a Federal Reserve System according to the Federal Reserve Act of 1913. It provided a system of stringent rules whereby banks could borrow and loan out Federal Reserve Notes.

The Federal Reserve was created to stabilize currency and gold values in compliance with an international gold standard, but such costs of World War I from 1914 to 1918 to fund military action persuaded many European nations to detach themselves from the gold standard. They gradually would recommit to it after the war during a time of prosperity in the USA until the Great Depression occurred in the 1930s that prolonged longer than any other.

As to why the Great Depression prolonged as long as it did in the USA, such monetarists as Milton Friedman and Anna J. Schwartz argued its main cause was a thirty-five percent monetary contraction resulting in deflation of prices, bankruptcies, unemployment and so on. Ben Bernanke, as Federal Reserve Chairman in 2002, agreed, and the British economist John Maynard Keynes had similarly argued recessions occur because of a lack of public spending.

The primary difference between the economists is their solutions. Friedman and Schwartz argued for a constant but gradual increase in the money supply to maintain a healthy inflation rate, whereas Keynes advocated an assistance of government for a healthy distribution of wealth, such as to employ workers on involuntary unemployment. Other means could be a policy of banks to impose a temporary redo of contracts resulting in too much debt. A postponement of mortgage payments during a recession to collect rent instead of payment on the principle, for instance, could prevent a great number of bankruptcies instead of banks having to foreclose on devalued property that is further vacated and devalued because of a lack of upkeep. Banks, potential buyers and renters could all benefit from such a change in banking policy.

Whether Keynesian or Monetarist policies were, or would have been, the more applicable or more detrimental to the recovery is conditional to the situation at hand. An analysis is here given for more understanding regarding circumstances relating to supply and demand economics and the economic policies in play after WWI and during the economic boom of the roaring twenties. However, it is first noted that actual experiences of the Great Depression are generally not included in the abstract analyses of economic policies.

It is not difficult for economists to examine abstract indications, as to therefore claim the initial recession would have been self-corrected in a fair amount of time, but the actual hardship experienced by countless victims of the depression was an economic tragedy to them. There is much testimony to such hardship: more than twenty thousand suicides; the homeless living in rusted-out cars or on park benches while using discarded newspapers for blankets in order to endure the cold;

children skipping school in helping the family out with meager paying jobs; one and a half million wives striving to make ends meet with low paying jobs after they were abandoned by jobless husbands; more than four-hundred thousand farms lost to bankruptcy, with other farmers burying their corn and wheat and dumping milk on roads rather than to sell them at a lower price; soup kitchens and long bread lines; illegally deporting Latino citizens born in the USA; last hired and first fired minority workers; a couple WWI military veterans killed for protesting with many others a veto by President Hoover of an early payment of a bonus promised according to a WWI Compensation Act of 1924. (The latter was also vetoed by President Franklin Delano Roosevelt. Congress overcame it to finally grant a nine-year early payment in 1936.) Although not all American citizens experienced a lot of hardship, those that did were not simply lazy or incompetent; they instead were victims of the monetary circumstances of the time.

One particular circumstance was how the gold standard influenced the economy after WWI. From WWI until 1929 the USA exports acquired from Europe provided a surplus of gold. By August 1929 the Federal Banks' gold reserves about doubled what the Federal Reserve Act of 1913 had required, as the USA accumulated about forty percent of the monetary gold of nations on the gold standard. The USA continued this hoarding trend of gold on into the depression whereby the USA and France had accumulated about sixty percent of the monetary gold supply. However, they both endured more of the depression. Such nations as China and Spain that were not on the gold standard experienced less depression. England and Scandinavian nations that abandoned the gold standard sooner recovered sooner from the depression. The policy of the gold standard act with regard to its implementation thus seems to have been flawed.

The founding of the Federal Reserve System in 1914 resulted from the Reserve Act of 1913. A main purpose of the system was to control money supply in circulation in order to prevent such banking panics as occurred in 1907. The primary means of control was in establishing an elastic currency in circulation that can be either increased or decreased to counter negative effects of price inflation and deflation of the general economy. The Federal Reserve was established having authority to issue Discount Notes to Federal Reserve Banks for them to discount them, in turn, to commercial banks and other financial institutions.

A Reserve Bank was required to maintain at least a forty percent gold reserve for outstanding public loans. To control dire inflation effects, as by authority of the Federal Reserve Controller, discount rates, as interest rates, were supposed to be increased to discourage public borrowing. With higher bank interest rates also paid to depositors' saving accounts, deposits would also compete against stock investments to also decrease the amount of money in circulation. The lowering of interest rates was supposed to apply with regard to adverse effects of deflation.

A criticism of the policy is that it was too restrictive to properly work during some dire situations. It only had temporary loan control, as lender of last resort, over member banks, but the number of state-chartered banks as members of the federal system was only ten percent in December of 1929. The ninety percent of nonmember banks held about twenty-five percent of all deposits to all national and state-chartered banks. The nonmember banks and other investment banking institutions were also allowed to speculate in stocks.

An error of judgment also occurred. In August of 1929, the Federal Board responded in finally approving a request by the Federal Reserve Bank of New York to raise interest rates. In response, foreign central banks raised their interest rates. Commercial banks of New York City became strained with a rise in reserve requirement as the stock market capital transferred into banks. There was a Stock Market crash on October 29, 1929. The Federal Reserve then responded by lowering interest rates to successfully reverse the recession. This occurrence provided an indication of how banking policy could affect the world economy along with other events of a tragic nature, whoever or whatever was at fault. However, other conditions emerging from the past were to have even more negative effect.

While the USA maintained the gold standard while European nations departed from it during WWI, USA benefited from its financing European war needs and its recovery after the war. After a minor recession occurred in the early twenties, the roaring twenties emerged as a period of prosperity. A Rich Class along with a Middle Class emerged. High wages were encouraged for the distribution of capital promoting spending and investment. A government budget became a surplus, and President Hoover successfully proposed in 1930 a reduction of taxes by one percent, but he subsequently proposed a large tax increase in 1931 in order to counter a budget deficit.

Although a Middle Class emerged in the 1920s, distribution of wealth was not proportionate. Average wages did not keep pace with profit, which resulted in less demand for products produced in 1929. In compliance with lower wages, farmers competed against each other, resulting in an increased supply and decreased price of harvest and livestock. As the price of farming equipment rose, farmers struggled even more. A worldwide surplus of food seemed to emerge to challenge the price of farming produce resulting from more efficient farming methods and new technology of modernized nations inclining to produce more for less. However, even though the data indicates there was food aplenty, the analysis is abstract, as applying only to whoever could have afforded the market value of the food. If true, then a counter to this deflationary trend could have been food stamps issued to the needy, as a temporary means to counter deflation and facilitate distribution of wealth, but other deflationary tactics were employed instead.

Farmers had also depleted nutrients of fertile topsoil that had taken more than a thousand years for nature to create. It swiftly became depleted by drought and strong winds in the summer of 1931. The Dust Bowl thus occurred in New Mexico, Oklahoma, Texas, Colorado and Kansas. With a lack of harvest to feed cattle in the fall of 1934, the government purchased and destroyed thousands of livestock in an attempt to stabilize stock prices. Total deflation, as including lower wages and so forth, could have been the natural means of adjustment, except loans for mortgages and so forth favor the loaner, not the borrower. The rich who hoard their wealth also become richer with regard to deflated prices, whereas investment becomes the trend in order to counter inflation. Destroying cattle to counter deflation likely contributed to the inability of the poor to afford the purchase of food instead.

Although a Middle Class emerged in the 1920s, distribution of wealth was not proportionate. Average wages did not keep pace with profit, which resulted in less demand for products produced in 1929. In compliance with lower wages, farmers competed against each other, resulting in an increased supply and decreased price of harvest and livestock. As the price of farming equipment rose, farmers struggled evermore. The Dust Bowl was somewhat of a relief to some farmers while it was devastation to many others.

Investment banks also speculated in the stock market. When the value of stocks declined, some banks did not have enough funds to legally operate in an effective manner. The largest financial institution of the southern states, for instance, was Caldwell and Company. In providing banking, brokerage and insurance coverage, it also lost a great amount of its capital reserve in stock investment. Following it, the Bank of New York ceased its operation. Credit became difficult to obtain. Hoarding money was more preferred. Prices of commodities declined. Many companies, including banks, closed. The poor became poorer because of higher levels of unemployment.

Hoover became President in March 1929. He proclaimed, in a 1930 State of the Union Address, "Prosperity cannot be restored by raids upon public Treasury". His Union Address statement is consistent with his commitment to a balanced budget. He vetoed several bills intending to provide relief for Americans in need of it, but he also proposed such projects as construction of the Hoover Dam. To pay for them, he approved tax increases and signed into law a record tariff, as the Smoot-Hawley Tariff in name. A balanced budget was achieved in 1931 along with a plummeting economy of about a twenty-five percent unemployment rate. Although prices deflated, wages did not, as for support of the remaining work force with the aid of unions.

In a limited way, Hoover initiated the New Deal Franklin D. Roosevelt proposed after becoming President in 1933. Under Hoover, included in the budget was additional revenue for national parks and forests along with the creation of the Veterans Administration, adding to the number of veteran hospital facilities. He signed the Davis-Bacon Act mandating that all federal funded construction projects pay an above average union wage to all employees. He further pleaded to business leaders to pay fair wages for increasing spending and preserving the overall health of the economy.

The remedies of Hoover were modest and restricted by law, leading to contraction of the money supply and a worst and more lasting depression. By 1933, the unemployment rate had risen above twenty-five percent in the industrial and mining regions of the economy. Farming income had become less than half of what it had been in 1929, and there was a closure of more than forty percent of eleven thousand national banks.

Bank runs were rapid. As Franklin Delano Roosevelt took office in March of 1933, state governors had declared bank holidays in order to postpone bank-runs. The most immediate concern of the President was thus the banking crises. On March 5, he declared a four-day holiday to prevent further withdrawals and closures.

Congress, on March 9, passed an Emergency Banking Act allowing the President to intervene during banking crises, as to reorganize banks, close insolvent ones, and to allow the twelve Federal Reserve Banks to issue additional currency as needed. With a plea by FDR for citizens to deposit their savings in the banks, three-fourths of the banks reopened by the end of the month. Bank security was further enhanced by a June 16 enactment of a Banking Act of 1933 for the establishment of the Federal Deposit Insurance Corporation. In addition, a Securities Act of 1933 was enacted as a means to help prevent stock market crashes. On April 19, 1933, by executive order, FDR temporarily removed the USA from the gold standard.

An Emergency Relief Administration that Hoover had created in 1932 was revised as the Federal Emergency Relief Administration, and it eventually became the Works Progress Administration in 1935. It along with a Civilian Conservation Corps allowed Federal loans to states and cities for employing unskilled workers in conservation and development of natural resources in rural lands owned by states, cities or the federal government. Development of a national infrastructure was also included as part of the New Deal for building roads, hydroelectric dams and so on. Farmers suffering from too low prices of harvest and livestock were provided relief by means of being paid for not producing. A Home Owner's Loan Act was also enacted. Congress amended Prohibition of Alcohol to allow brewing of a beer industry, and a National Recovery Act guaranteed worker the right to organize as a union to bargain for fair wages and working conditions. A national labor board was established by executive order along with the Civil Works Administration to provide work for about four million unemployed workers during the winter months of 1933 and 1934. On June 28, 1934 the National Housing Act (FHA) allowed the Housing Administration to insure loans for construction or repair of homes. On August 14, 1935 FDR signed the Social Security Act that guaranteed pensions to retirees sixty-five years of age, and it provided financial aid to dependent children and the blind, establishing unemployment insurance as well.

Some of these acts had both positive and negative effects. Labor unions can benefit workers with higher wages and better working conditions; they can also lead to unemployment and bankruptcy if companies cannot afford the change. Paying to not produce food crops can benefit farmers; it can also prevent the purchase of food by those in need of it.

As was Hoover, FDR also was a proponent of a balanced budget. Some of the New Deal reforms were intended as temporary measures. Because of an improvement of the banking system towards 1935, the early bonus payment bill to WWI veterans was vetoed, but the Congress, Senate and key advisers of the administration that FDR had fortunately inherited were more willing to enact reform. Congress overrode the veto.

Those who favored New Deal Reforms became referred to as liberals. Those who opposed them became known as conservatives. The liberals had dominated, but conservatives were favored in mid elections between 1933 and 1935 due to such controversies as with regard to unionization.

The economy improved towards 1937, but only temporarily, as the recession continued. Meanwhile, FDR concentrated on preparing for war. Congress had passed Neutrality Acts in 1935 and 1936 prohibiting exports for military war needs and the extension of credit to any nation considered inclined to war, but FDR was more in tune with an upcoming threat of another world war threat by Germany.

Germany's economy and military, second only to the USA in 1914, were devastated by 1918 due to WWI. By treaty, Germany was obligated to pay victims reparations for its war damages. Because it was unable to pay the compensation, France and Belgium invaded Germany in 1921 to strip it of its goods and raw materials. During 1923, Germany experienced hyperinflation by printing fiat money in order to pay striking workers. However, Germany became extremely prosperous and peaceful from 1924 to 1929 due to the gracious credit of the USA. However, in the final two months of 1929, gold reserves of the USA were in decline, and the USA requested Germany pay off its debt owed to the USA. Perhaps this reverse policy, in part, aided an Adolf Hitler political platform of hate.

In 1937 and 1938, the USA economy was in decline, but it stabilized in 1939 and began to soar in 1940 with an export of European war needs. The USA gold supply that began increasing in 1938 increased more rapidly in 1940 with a German invasion into France. The increased USA money supply was countered by investing in rearmament. Lower priced bonds were sold that rendered more public investment. Taxes were increased, but mandatory rationing aided with the issuance of coupons that countered the threat of rapid inflation is testimony that the cost of public service can benefit the overall economy besides what the money is used to produce.

A Lend-Lease program of the USA also supplied allied nations, along with a French resistance force against Germany, with food, oil and other material needs. Subsequently, leaders of nations gathered in Bretton Woods, New Hampshire of the USA, in 1945, to establish the Bretton Wood (International Monetary Fund) policy whereby individual countries are to maintain a one percent exchange rate variance of the gold standard in promoting monetary cooperation and financial stability to facilitate international trade, promote employment, sustain economic growth, and to reduce poverty. A Marshall Plan was later implemented in the USA to help finance the recovery of Europe.

A foreign aid policy followed. USA charity dollars provided incentive for importing USA products, as to increase employment and positive distribution of wealth among USA citizens. Give and receive was the outcome. To cut off all that aid would more likely have resulted in a grave outcome of economic disruption.

During the war, the USA experienced some budget deficits, but overall there was a positive result in the redistribution of wealth. After the war, the rate of inflation was modest for decades with low interest rates encouraging such investment as in housing among a Middle Class enjoying the American Dream. In the latter half of the century, the distribution of wealth tended to once again benefit the wealthiest, as to again lead to a fragile economy that was prone to a recession in the twenty first century.

By 1960 the USA held nineteen and two-fifths billion dollars in gold reserves, which included one and three-fifths billion as an International Monetary Fund, to render it with eighteen and seven-tenths billion to cover foreign dollars outstanding. However, as the USA economy prospered, Americans bought more imported goods, paying in USA dollars. A balance of payment deficit worried foreign governments that the USA would no longer back up the dollar in gold. By 1970, the USA held fourteen and a half billion of its gold reserve against its foreign dollar holdings of fifteen and seven-tenths billion. On August 15, 1971, by order of President Nixon, the gold ratio to the dollar was changed from thirty-five to thirty-eight dollars per ounce, and the Federal Reserve was no longer allowed to redeem dollars with gold. The USA raised gold to forty-two dollars per ounce in 1973, and decoupled from the gold standard altogether in 1976.

The monetary value of the dollar is now simply whatever it can purchase. Although gold can still be used to compare values of different currencies among nations, it is not needed as such. Consider marbles instead as representative of various products in general. In accordance with domestic demand, if the USA producers produce ten marbles at a dollar cost to sell for ten dollars, and producers in France produce ten marbles at a cost of ten francs that sell for one hundred francs, then ten francs equates to the value of a dollar. The comparison is relatively the same whether marbles or gold. Moreover, if France doubles its printed amount of currency in circulation, then twenty francs become worth a USA dollar. Providing population and productive capacity both remain the same for both France and the USA, and providing the USA is capable of adjusting to the change in value of the franc, a fiat money standard allows nations more flexibility to adjust to their domestic situations than does a limited amount of gold reserve.

Fiat money as credit is a facilitator for economic wealth. However, its application is more complex. Along with the Federal Reserve needing to control the amount of money in circulation, as to prevent negative effects of inflation followed by deflation, there are stock market investments competing against bonds, bank interest rates, and investments in commodities. The Federal Reserve lowers the prime interest rate during periods of recession. Without government bonds and other securities to invest in, the only game left for money earning money is from stock dividends that can continually increase along with an increase in value of the stocks. However, the payment of dividends in voluntary and it becomes costlier for whatever production the stock represents.

During and after the recession beginning in 2008, the Federal Reserve has been waiting for inflation to occur before increasing the prime interest rate. No such inflation occurred even though there was a substantial increase in National Debt. What needs to occur is an even and fair distribution of wealth for ample opportunity for all of us to succeed in life and experience the American Dream. It could have occurred sooner with more government investing in the infrastructure. Such investment would reduce unemployment, create social wealth along with economic wealth, trend towards higher wages for the competitive need of workers in the private sector, and thus result in a healthy rate of inflation to raise interest rates to balance out the competitive edge of the stock market and those of any of us with extreme wealth.

# 10

## INFLATION DEFLATION ECONOMICS

## AVOIDING RECESSION

Deflation after a period of inflation is generally considered a critical part of whatever causes economic recession. For instance, a recession beginning in 2009 has been claimed to have been caused by a housing bubble along with a too lenient policy of bank lending. The too lenient lending policy consisted of insecure loans whereby a ratio of home buyer debt to available income of buyers gained fifty percent from 1990 to 2007. Along with this result an increase in housing prices peaked in early 2006 to become lower in 2007. In effect, the increased interest rates along with too lenient loaning led to bankruptcies of the banking system as well as borrowers who could no longer afford paying back loans. The fourth largest financial firm in the USA, Lehman Brothers, filed Chapter Eleven Bankruptcy Protection on September 15, 2009. It was the start of a worldwide trend of deflated pricing due to less credit available for the circulation of the money supply.

The purpose here is to explain how a particular balance of consumable product and monetary circulation can avoid a recession and promote prosperity. Such product includes a distinction between economic wealth and social wealth as part of a functional balance. Social wealth includes the quality of air we breathe that has little, if any, or even negative economic value. It is here proposed that investing in a healthy environment in a particular way can also contribute to the production of economic wealth as a positive part of social wealth.

What constitutes wealth? It had been measured in the past by a gold standard. However, the measure of wealth is actually in the eye of the beholder, being actual product instead of gold or some other kind of currency.

Some proponents of a gold standard argue the principle cause of inflation is the liberal printing of fiat currency. A counter argument is hoarding of gold leads to deflation and the accumulation of wealth by its hoarders. With less gold currency in circulation, lower prices of goods occur from which the hoarders of gold have more purchasing ability because of lower prices due to less demand from less money available to purchase. The greed for gold power might very well have led to wars.

The deflation argument is not without precedence. As to why a Great Depression prolonged as long as it did in the 1930s, such monetarists as Milton Friedman and Anna J. Schwartz argued its main cause was a thirty-five percent monetary contraction that resulted in the deflation of prices, bankruptcies, unemployment and so forth. Ben Bernanke, as the Federal Reserve Chairman beginning in 2002, agreed, and the British economist John Maynard Keynes had previously argued recessions occur because of a lack of public spending.

The primary difference between the economists is their solutions. Friedman and Schwartz argued a gradual increase in money supply for gradual inflation promotes spending, as for investing in commodities before they increase price, whereas Keynes' solutions that applied to the Great Depression advocated government should assist in attaining a healthy distribution of wealth by employing those on involuntary unemployment. The latter is sometimes hyperbolized as socialism by political bias even though the former is also a social government solution, supposedly supporting free enterprise.

Gradual inflation can instigate investment, but the effects of inflation and deflation are more complex. Aspects regarding recession are here considered according to supply and demand economics.

A non-inflation-non-deflation-economy can occur if supply and demand maintain a particular balance. If there is an increase in population for more demand of product, then more products produced are for more purchases. If currency is only proportionately distributed among customers at a particular average rate, then there becomes less of it spent per person regarding an increase in population along with an increase in the number of products to sell. Prices usually need to be lowered in order to sell additional product to additional customers. To avoid deflation, either more currency needs to be added to the distribution of it or the rate of spending needs to increase. The circulation of currency is thus credit that, in effect, facilitates the production of product as either economic or social wealth.

More money for spending with not enough products to satisfy demand can lead to inflation. Ideally, avoiding both inflation and deflation requires respective decreases or increases of currency in circulation. It could result from either credit and debit cards speeding up the process or more currency in circulation being notes of credit that are printed by the Federal Treasury as National Debt. Ideally, the same changes in supply and demand, and the amount of currency in circulation per person results in no reason for either inflation or deflation to occur.

An increase in product per person can itself lead to deflation of prices, as evident of an oil surplus with the additional use of solar energy. Effects resulting from such a surplus are extensively complex. A decrease in gasoline prices can further cheapen prices of goods being transported to stores, as to stimulate more purchase of more demand, and it could even allow for an increase in wages if an increase in profit is shared accordingly. However, the demand for employment can also be a determining factor of wage growth. If unemployment is high, the profit could be kept by ownership. if there is then cause for higher wages and employment for more distribution of wealth in the overall economy, then a mandatory increase in wage by government might be beneficial for a more robust economy overall for that particular circumstance.

Inflation is more likely to occur with a mandatory minimum wage increase by government action. Higher wages along with cheaper gasoline prices for lower production cost of product can benefit the low wage earner. It can, in turn, increase product along with its greater demand by the general public, but a trade imbalance between nations can also occur until the monetary values of foreign and domestic currencies adjust to whatever the monetary value of product actually is to each nation.

Although it is argued that the hoarding of gold has led to deflation and the accumulation of wealth by the hoarders, fiat currency is also hoarded by being deposited in savings accounts with little or no intent for present spending on the open market, as by either the one with the savings account or no additional loaning by the banks. Simply investing in stocks for future retirement income can similarly reduce the quantity of money supply in circulation, depending on how the investment is used at the time. For instance, if it is used by people of higher income, their competing for a particular work of art could inflate its price while such essentials as food and shelter for the needy deflate below the cost of production for less of it to become available. As for a counter, food stamps for the needy can be a means to circulate a more general form of credit from which farmers could profit from more production of it.

When such hoarding of money leads to a recession, there is an "easing" policy applied by the Federal Reserve for increasing the amount of money in circulation, which is more freely applied internationally with the use of fiat currency than changing the price of gold according to a gold standard. There was thus an attempt to counter deflation of the 2009 recession by the Central Bank system selling such government securities as bonds of a lower interest rate to commercial banks for them to loan, in turn, at a lower interest rate to the general public. However, the Federal Reserve interest rates from the 2009 recession approached zero, which became the limit of quantitative easing. Since banks also paid less interest on deposits by the general public, the near zero interest rates by both the Federal Reserve and the banks became countered by investment in stocks. As stocks became the more popular alternative, their values increased along with the dividend income per stock, as granted by the heads of companies supposedly for a more attractive stock investment. With banks paying little or no interest on savings deposits, and there being little if any other long-term investment opportunity for future growth and financial security, banks having less capital to loan is likely why the Federal Reserve easing policy for countering deflation became itself countered as such.

Note: it is supposedly unlawful for a company to sell shares of it as stocks, use the money to invest in other stocks, and then file bankruptcy, leaving its stockholders in debt. Government policy of control thus includes the stock market as well.

Rigorous loaning restrictions are another factor contributing to deflation and a slower recovery from recession. Although interest rates are lowered to help recover from a recession, banks become less willing to loan. The unwillingness to loan is not merely because a thirty-year low interest rate could result in loss of opportunity of a higher interest rate in the near future, as banks need to loan for them to generate income and pay expenses; it is mainly because there are stricter loaning conditions required of such financial institutions as banks during a recession. There is more risk during a period of recession that borrowers will be unable to pay back banks for their loans, as there tends to be more bankruptcies instead.

A wiser alternative to bankruptcies could be a temporary suspension of high mortgage payments in favor of affordable rent instead by extending the remaining contract to a future date of economic recovery. It could prevent the decline in values of non-occupied homes occurring because of their lack of upkeep.

How, then, does government help the economy recover from a recession?

One possible way is the Keynesian method of government increasing opportunity for employment. Government employment generally pays more along with better working conditions than do private companies taking advantage of competitive employment. However, the general effect on the economy is dependent on supply and demand conditions. Government revenue by way of taxing wages and other earnings for government services constitutes a flow of the money supply. If the services, in the eyes of its receivers, are considered more valuable than what would otherwise be created by the private sector, then social wealth is enhanced by social conformity. If the government services are less valuable in the eyes of the beholders than what can be produced by the private sector, then the tax is a deterrent to the innovation of economic wealth creation.

It is argued that a democratic role of government is not to compete with free enterprise, but it is allowed to create social wealth instead of economic wealth. However, there are a few exceptions to consider. If additional non-competitive wealth is created along with an increase in the money supply by flow, there is simply additional distribution of money having more ability to further provide incentive for producers to produce the same number of products as economic wealth. Similarly, if additional product equal to additional demand counterbalances an additional money supply, then neither inflation nor deflation need occur. However, if government favors solar energy over man-made carbon fuels, then it could counter free enterprise to result in deflation of prices because of government product replacing free enterprise product, but social product combined with economic product as total wealth can sometimes be more prosperous than merely producing economic wealth alone.

A difference between social wealth and economic wealth is that social wealth can be environmental. The air we breathe is essential to our well-being, but it has little if any economic value since its abundance is relatively free according to supply and demand. It even has negative economic value to companies that are required to either prevent or clean up their pollution of it. However, if the tax on air pollution is only used to clean it up, then social wealth created is only a non-competitive wealth in addition to economic wealth. The issue of concern then becomes whether the polluters or the general public should pay the expenses resulting from the pollution. Ideally, one way or the other would help maintain a better distribution in the flow of the money supply as credit for other purchases, but a tax on polluters could also help deter their polluting in the first place if it does not also render the production of product too expensive to produce.

If the cost of cleaning up air pollution is by a government tax, then a faster circulation of money increased by way of credit could lead to deflation, inflation or neither. The latter could be because of an appropriate increase in employment. However, even though there is a social product being created out of tax revenue to automatically balance supply and demand, the tax might not be evenly shared. With the increase in demand being social along with additional tax revenue, wages need to increase along with the price of product. More economic credit is thus required, as by the Federal Reserve increasing the money supply. A tax thus needs to be balanced out with an increase in the National Debt as printed money or debit-credit.

As for economic wealth, money is its measure, but the measure is according to the amount of product money is used to purchase commodities. If a dollar can be traded for a loaf of bread, then the dollar is worth a loaf of bread. In this sense, there can be a strategy in place were social wealth becomes economic wealth as well.

The creation of social wealth can be beneficial to the economy. More livable conditions can increase economic value of local property. As for government contribution, the construction of highways and railroads has enabled an increase in traffic for the shipment of goods and for the ease of travel by citizens. Investing in the Grand Coulee Dam in the state of Washington during the Great Depression assisted the growth of a farming community with water and electricity to spare. Investing more in the infrastructure of the roads, bridges and so forth could further increase economic wealth. Otherwise, future cost of repair will be left as a debt for our grandchildren to finance. In the same sense, more countering of present climate change could be beneficial to our grandchildren as well as the present benefit of employing the creative ability of those learned of more innovative technology to combat climate change.

Both economic wealth and social wealth are the measure of product itself instead of money. Money is only debit-credit for product. If production decreases and population increases, then even those receiving social security benefits will even become poorer. Although the amount of money for social security benefits increases with inflation, as by law for retirees to maintain their purchasing abilities, the incentive of workers to produce could be encumbered. With too much decrease in supply of products to satisfy demand, retiree income would eventually become entangled in the general competitive need to survive. On the other hand, if the social investment in flow of traffic and communication benefits production of product as well, then the social benefits are justifiable.

Another argument against government finance is that too much taxation causes a trade imbalance between nations. Even though investing in the infrastructure and technology can lead to an economic advantage of more production and satisfied demand for the distribution of local wealth, large corporations tend to transfer the production of their products to foreign nations with cheaper labor cost if their own government is financed by a higher progressive tax of the higher income level. For instance, if automobile producers move their operations to Mexico and China because of less circulation of local currency of the open market, then the domestic purchase of more automobiles from foreign producers can lead to an unbalance of trade.

An increase in the distribution of domestic currency by an increase in National Debt could help avoid a recession, but it would only be a temporary effect while foreign nations adjusted to the change in value of each currency. However, if increases in National Debt are an increase in the money supply, as government credit for additional production from shared public cost, then the affordable demand of product would be satisfied instead, as the National Debt is fundamentally internal debt financing production of wealth.

A controversial issue of concern is regarding that of trade and taxation. Companies paying higher domestic tax tend towards tax evasion. An automobile company in the USA, for instance, could technically affiliate with a company in Mexico for less taxation of profit. The USA Federal government once taxed the income of such affiliates, but it no longer does. The USA government thus receives no tax from the affiliate that pays less tax to Mexico.

Tax evasion is more common with a progressive tax system. Although larger companies benefit from efficiency of operation of selling to a larger population, they still compete among foreign companies paying less tax to their native country. A proportionate tax to income would internally balance out for credit of purchase to remain the same, but the result is more complex if the tax rate increases with higher income. Overall, it could either be a positive outcome for evening out the distribution of wealth and elimination of monopolies and oligopolies or it could be a negative outcome if it renders exports to expensive in comparison to foreign competition.

Trade among nations can itself be either beneficial or detrimental. If nations have laws and/unions for fairer working conditions and/or for healthier or more reliable product, then its trade with the less restrictive nation could result in less quality of domestic production. A benefit of foreign trade is that nations differing in demand for certain domestic products can more efficiently satisfy the general populous more efficiently. China, for instance, has an abundance of previous metals for such high technology used in national defense, whereas the USA has a more favorable environment for agriculture. Trade entanglements could also either result in disputes and war or more cooperative dependence on each other for world peace. With the vast difference in laws of nations there are no easy solutions, but overall differences generally only have minor short-term effects. Long term effects could be why the reputation of quality products has declined over the years. I once purchased rubber boots from Sears made in the USA that I still where after more than fifty years. Boots I purchased that were made in China leaked the first night I wore them to work.

With an increase in the money supply there can also be inflation of the domestic price of goods and a decrease in exports along with a deficit from international trade. However, although an increased money supply can devalue the dollar, as to decrease the ability of foreigners to purchase American products with such currency, leading to National Debt of trade imbalance, it is only temporary. In due time, the cheaper dollar will adjust to that of foreign currency. In effect, the cheaper dollar is counter to recession, as evident of the faster recovery from the Great Depression by nations temporary abandoning the Gold Standard sooner than other nations abandoned it.

Increasing the money supply can cheapen the dollar to which other nations adjust. After their adjustment, a trade balance is restored by there being higher prices per dollar on both imports and deports. However, if the increase in money supply is used to produce additional purchasable product, whereby inflation need not occur, then there can be an increase in economic wealth from a trade imbalance that rebalances according to tax and Federal Reserve credit policy.

In order not to interfere with free enterprise in an unfair manner, a more responsible role of government is for it to assist in the creation of social wealth. However, social wealth often conflicts with economic wealth. For the sake of the economy, the role of government should also be to balance the creation of social wealth with the creation of economic wealth.

Creation of social wealth by government generally involves taxation that can also be balanced by an increase in the money supply. If government immediately spends its tax revenue for public benefit, then circulation of the money supply is increased as much as well. If the government spends the money for a rocket expedition to Mars, then there is no competitive interference with free enterprise. The real issue of concern is whether not environmental concerns can be more beneficial to social and economic wealth combined.

# 11

# LAW AND ORDER

# OF

# MONETARY FREEDOM

What is the value of money?

There are two particular values. One of them is the enhanced convenience to purchase goods and services. If a loaf of bread costs a dollar, then the dollar equates to whatever value that particular loaf of bread is to the customer. However, money not only permits us to choose what particular type of bread or something else to purchase, it further entails a sense of freedom in that there is more extensive value of money empowering us with more convenience of how we choose to live our lives.

In choosing how to live our lives, part of our freedom is spent along with the purchase of product, as there is then need to earn more money to maintain our freedom of choice. Conformity is thus a counterpart of financial freedom. Similarly, if we can choose who to marry, the success of it generally depends on how we conform to conditions more favorable to the lifestyles by which both partners prefer to live.

Conformity is a counterpart of freedom, but the freedom aspect of the economy seems more favorable. Those of us with more money and the freedom to spend it are more preferred by the general public depending on income for their livelihood. Social wealth, such as a more livable environment, is thus more in denial. The denial, however, is subjective. If it is able to create opportunity for participation in the creation of appreciable wealth, either economic or social, then it can become more acceptable.

Conformity as commitment to choose is the flip side of freedom. With danger becoming too great to overcome by single individuals, we are inclined to join together to agree on rules of conduct, as to partner among ourselves a more favorable game of life to combat forces beyond our individual control. This later tendency escalates to more government, as among nations having nuclear capability to destroy life here on Earth as we know it.

Whatever the rules, ideally, they are acceptable to all of us. However, rules are only preferred if they allow participation in the game of life. A military is acceptable inasmuch as it defends our wealth. Although climate change is somewhat less acceptable, it is also a threat to our wealth, not only to the USA, but to the world in general. Global participation to counter climate change even has the potential of obtaining peace and worldwide prosperity by bringing us together for a worthy cause.

We compete to survive. In general, survival is a twofold strategy. We compete individually by means of self-determination, but we unite as an organized community as well in order to survive more difficult obstacles that require more cooperation among us. The latter strategy more often than not requires enforceable rules of conduct, as our individual needs and preferences are often contrary to the needs of society at large. Some of us cheat and violate the law. Enforcing the law requires finance. If lawfulness is not enforced, then cheating on the rules becomes an advantage to the cheaters for chaos being apt to prevail.

Government invests in a police force and a military to enforce law and order and protect against invasion. The investment in roads and the general infrastructure has been beneficial to the economy. More social investment in climate change solutions could also be an economic benefit of the future. It could also be a present benefit by countering recession from deflation by providing employment for maintaining the distribution of wealth.

What needs to occur for governmental compliance to climate change is a compromise of solutions. Investing in solar energy is one part of the compromise, investing in technology for cleaner use of carbon fuels is another part. As for the latter alternative, carbon contributes to climate change only if it is absorbed in the atmosphere. If it can be kept from being absorbed into the atmosphere, then it can be economically used without negative consequence to the environment. Thus, if government further invests equally in solar energy and cleaner uses of carbon energy, then it would have more support from beneficial entrepreneurs of the policy

To reiterate, money has value in itself as a convenient means of exchanging goods and services. In a psychological sense, it empowers us with the freedom to choose what goods and services to purchase. Even though it is possible to exchange an apple for a loaf of bread, the convenience of the dollar empowers us with more ability to live our lives according to our preferences. However, contained in the game of life is another element called competition. Having more money to spend does not further power us if everyone else has it as well. Actual wealth is product instead of money. Only if there are more products available to purchase with the greater amount of money is our freedom to purchase them enhanced. Freedom to spend thus depends on the available amount of product we can purchase with our money. Otherwise, inflation deflates the value of the more money we have to spend because of relatively higher prices of products countering the increased money supply.

What guarantee does money have as an acceptable means of exchange for goods and services?

Such money as gold was originally representative of the goods and services circulating among the general population of society. The gold as collateral of money used to represent it had simply been used for the trade of those goods and services, which are essentially the real collateral in support of the value of the currency

Gold was also regarded as more viable collateral in that it was also considered to have a value according to the amount of labor required to discover and produce it as equal to the cost of labor or whatever the gold could be purchased for. However, when gold was hoarded, or circulated out of the country, less money rendered a period of deflation that rendered the hoarder of gold more economically wealthy, except for a decrease in productivity also rendering a relatively more overall poverty of society to offset the individual increase in economic wealth to particular individuals. For entrepreneurs to sell there needs to be enough distribution of credit among customers in order for them to afford their purchases. An uneven distribution of wealth can otherwise be a deterrent to prosperity for both the employee and the entrepreneur.

Even though the gold standard has by many of us been considered more of a guarantee of economic wealth, its value is still only relative. To someone in the desert needing water to survive, a canteen of water is more essential to life than a ton of gold. Similarly, the air we breathe is more critical for sustaining our lives, even though it has no economic value except for a negative one if industry is required to clean up their air pollution.

Money today is fiat. Instead of it being backed by gold, it is issued and regulated according to Federal Reserve policy as constitutive of governmental authority. Gold is thus no longer accepted by government as the official means of exchange for goods and services, and we citizens generally accept the fiat currency for its convenience value of purchasing product aplenty if so produced.

Even though money has a convenience value, as fiat or otherwise, it is still determined by whatever it can be exchanged for. For product aplenty, the dollar is worth more than if products are scarcer. If food becomes scarce, then its cost increases along with competition, as according to the economic law known as supply and demand whereby a general supply of product with lesser demand is priced lower compared to a scarce product of relatively more demand. This principle, in itself, suggests a motivation to produce more favorable products. However, the value of money is only economic, as subjective to the cost of living. In contrast, the air we breathe has more social value than economic value. The social value of air is taken for granted because of its freedom to breathe it whereas economic value only constitutes the desire to exercise our freedom to spend the money on whatever empowers the money in determining the state of the economy.

The value of money is also speculative, but we are gamblers by nature. The risk of losing money in a poker game excites us similar to how a more dangerous and challenging life seems to render our lives more meaningful. The self-risk of life, such as to climb the tallest mountain, is a challenge for bragging rights. However, freedom often becomes too much of a challenge. In the Old Wild West free of law and order, for instance, James Butler (Wild Bill) Hickok (1837-1876) was shot in the back by a disgruntled poker loser. The alleged killer was tried and found innocent by a jury in the lawless town of Deadwood, but he was later retried and found guilty of murder by a jury in a more lawful town nearby. Such a happening is a typical societal trend. Even though many of us still yearn for a freer and challenging way of life, more law and order also seem preferred by many of us in a more populous area of opposing ideas for a safer community in which to live. In western movies, for instance, it was common for towns to outlaw the possession of guns because of a tendency of cowboys herding cows to market drank too much alcohol and ended up using their guns in disputes. People with less ability to defend themselves were more in need of a police force.

Conformity and commitment are the flip sides of freedom. We are more inclined to agree on rules of conduct whenever danger becomes too great to overcome by single individuals, as for us to partner among ourselves a more favorable game of life to combat forces beyond individual control. Generally, denser populations of people with more controversial issues seem to accept enforcement of a more lawful and orderly way of life. The tendency escalates on up to more government, as among nations having nuclear capability to destroy life here on Earth as we know it.

What rules do we choose to play by?

Whatever the rules, ideally, they are acceptable to all of us. However, the old cliché that rules are made to be broken applies. Rules in the competitive world are only preferred if they entail participation in the game of life. To agree on outlawing the proliferation of nuclear weapons is acceptable inasmuch as the threat of a holocaust is a self-deterrent, but it is generally taken for granted insofar as the general public has no vote on the policy. If life is destroyed, so be it; we live our lives accordingly. We compete in this world to survive it. In general, survival consists of a twofold strategy. We compete individually by means of self-determination, but we unite as an organized community in order to survive more difficult obstacles, which require cooperation and trust among us. The latter strategy more often than not requires enforceable rules of conduct, as our individual needs and preferences are often contrary to the needs of society at large. For instance, earning an income is more preferable to some of us than the unknowing threat of climate change. Present employment is thus prioritized in denial of environmental concerns of future consequences.

What matters most in a Democracy by the people for the people is the participation of the people for the determination of a most acceptable game of life in which to play. The participation is competitive due to the differences in the needs and preferences of the people. In result, we have only a partial say in the outcome of majority rule of democracy. It could be a mere vote for a representative of our preference, or it could include a financial contribution of purchasing a product that persuades a particular outcome. Economics is thus a political factor in the sense it helps determine the game of life.

Although economics is experienced by participation, the role of government in deciding economic policy is political. Politics with its controversial debates on public policy more easily attracts our attention. However, spending money is still a means of political participation. What we choose to purchase is a vote on a particular product that producers of it compete to sell. The circulation of money simply allows a more convenient means of transactions to facilitate more production. Moreover, people with money are more welcomed than people without it, as spending creates incentive to produce and sell more products, which further creates jobs and economic wealth with enough innovation to succeed.

To the contrary of innovation is tradition and resistance to change. Even though the game of life includes economics, an economic role of government is politically controversial. Political conservatives advocate the private sector of free enterprise needs to be allowed to prosper with a least amount of governmental influence, but progressives point out instead government has a useful role in promoting a healthy economy along with social entitlements and a favorable environment. The point of issue is with regard to what constitutes the least amount of governmental influence in favor of the most preferable game of life. Although there appears to be a moderate view somewhere in between extremes for possible compromise, the extremism still factors in. Entitlements are more preferred by some of us whereas the more established of us are inclined to oppose policy of more distribution of wealth if it threatens their economic status in the community. Even investment to combat climate change for a better future for our grandchildren is often opposed by those of us involved in polluting the environment for profit and maintaining the status quo.

Entitlements can either have a positive or negative effect. There is the 'use it or lose it' tendency whereby some of us entitled, such as by employment in the U.S. Forest Service, merely produce to maintain status, but the outcome can still be positive in maintaining a healthy forest environment with camping facilities, and having them along Social Security, parks, other camping areas, and so forth are examples of social wealth created for more of us to have.

A check on the 'use it or lose it' tendency could be public opinion if the public is informed of what their taxation is spent for. Economic competition can also have either a positive or negative effect. There is cheating among competitors. Competing inspires innovation for creation of product, but the game of life ends if one player wins out over the rest of us. There is also cheating among competitors, and the wealthier among us who can hire more expensive lawyers have somewhat of an advantage in getting away with it.

Too much change in a short period of time, such as suddenly having more ways of obtaining available knowledge, can also be disastrous for us. With free information on the World Wide Web, for instance, self-education could eventually render universities and professors obsolete, as to counter a past and common trend of investing a great amount of effort for a more informative way of life. Although change is often necessary, it is generally more favorable if it is gradual enough to leave its victims ample time to adjust to it.

Change often threatens the establishment. If the change is due to free and fair competition, it generally becomes, in due time, more acceptable. However, if the change is due to government policy, there is generally more resistance to it, even if it provides more benefits to the general population at large. In the past, when there was not as much law enforcement in Eastern Oregon, it was common for ranchers to kill deer for no other reason than to prevent them from consuming grass needed for cattle to graze on. Nowadays, the enforcement of law threatens any of us accustomed to the freedom to kill deer at will, and there is estimated to be a lot more deer now than there was in past centuries.

There is preferred resistance to government action. Cigarette smokers become upset with government advertisement revealing cancerous effects from too much hazardous smoke in the lungs. The pleasure of smoking, no matter the risk, is individual choice, even if the choice ends in early death from painful cancer, even from second hand smoke from other smokers, and even if it results in expensive medical care at the expense of the taxpayer. Although it is also a Democratic choice of the majority to live according to rule of law, choosing the pleasure of smoking at the expense of others still remains a political threat to some of us. It can also be a threat to industry inasmuch as poor health renders more employment to doctors than employment of nutritionists. However, nowadays doctors seem more informed on nutritional benefits than they were in the past. It even seems possible their nutritional expertise could help bring down health care cost.

The economic and political establishment nowadays upheld by conservatives is the private sector of the economy thrives by competition that promotes products, as government entitlements only lead to a welfare state with little incentive to help create a prosperous economy. Conservatives further argue taxation for social welfare raises cost of production, as for more expensive exports that are more difficult to sell, such that the cheaper labor abroad results in more unemployment within the economy of higher cost of production. In this sense, they argue that the cost of too many entitlements will leave our grandchildren in debt.

A counterargument is that producers primarily have their own interest at stake, which can but need not benefit the interests of the general public. Sometimes worthwhile products are produced in increasing economic wealth of society as a whole; sometimes the self-interest of producers leads to less total wealth of society. Cattle ranchers, for instance, can lessen production of land for decades if they selfishly overgraze their cattle on it, which could potentially, even if unknowingly, lead to starvation of future generations of people, thus leaving our grandchildren with less wealth. For the benefit of the whole of society it is sometimes necessary to impose restrictions on individual land use regarding future concerns of environmental wealth. For further instance, tight water restrictions in some areas of New Mexico render a limited number of wells drilled in order to preserve more water for the general public.

Who decides what constitutes the economic game of life?

We have elected officials. Supposedly they serve the interest of voters. If a majority of voters is in favor of a law requiring more secure containers of medical remedies lest some spiteful individuals buy, poison and then put them back on store shelves, then the wise politician in office favors the enactment of a law for concealing containers for them to be more difficult to tamper with. The game of life thus tends to be planned according to rule of majority. However, majority rule often conflicts with individual freedom, as it sometimes miscalculates what constitutes a more prosperous future.

A critical factor in what constitutes the economic game of life is simply knowledge. Knowing better how to play cards might have enabled Wild Bill Hickok to be a winner, although it eventually led to his death. Knowing how to properly use land to preserve its future yield can render more opportunity for future wealth. A secret food recipe could render the producer of it a fortunate income. Knowing stock market tendencies more thoroughly could provide valuable insight for also achieving economic wealth. Although these are examples of individual innovation in view of competition, the social factor of education promotes an even more competitive approach to them having a more productive success. Moreover, more qualified officials could be elected to office if voters are more aware of the appropriate skills of the candidates, and so on, depending on public access to their qualifications.

Such early leaders as Thomas Jefferson were aware of the dependence of knowledge in promoting the welfare of our nation. They advocated that public education can be beneficial to both individuals and the whole of society. However, there are gaps among us in our levels of knowledge. As a secret recipe provides an advantage of one individual to be more successful, it is superior knowledge of certain political leaders that enable them with a more successful means of becoming elected to office. However, knowledge can also include the ability to fool the general public. If the general public is easily fooled, then it elects less qualified leaders for the real public interest. It is thus not merely our duty to vote; it is our duty to vote wisely. In this regard, the potential threat of global warming as essential for direction of a preferable game of life, as to promote both economic and social wealth, needs to be understood as such by society in general.

# 12

# FINANCING

# ECONOMIC CLIMATE CHANGE

Product is wealth instead of money itself. Extensive wealth was created agriculturally in allowing the development of modern day civilization with food aplenty. For instance, it allowed for the creation of such structures as the Great Pyramid of Egypt, and it has allowed for education for the development of such technology whereby manual labor has been replaced by machines and is gradually becoming replaced by computerized robots.

Distribution of economic wealth is now primarily according to ownership and skill for the use of technology (except for the threat of revolution if laws of the land favor too much of the rich instead of the poor). There is also the threat of climate change because of productive use of carbon fuel surpassing conditions of balance required to maintain a healthy environment. There is thus need to conform.

Average temperature is gradually rising. How can we reverse it? Heat is energy. We simply need to use the energy in a way that it does not readily recycle back as heat. However, using solar energy for economic benefits beyond individual achievement requires social solutions. A water and electric utility of a city or county can purchase electricity produced from solar panels only by affording it by charging a fee for its use. Otherwise, the solar energy needs to be as free as the air we breathe for the maintaining of social wealth as a healthy environment in which to live.

Financial solutions to climate change are distinguishable as by individual choice and social capitalism. By free choice, individuals simply purchase such solar energy apart from carbon fuels as electric vehicles and solar panels. Although many individuals avoid fossil fuels because of their devotion to the climate change cause, such individual solutions still compete financially with carbon fuels. Social solutions are still needed.

Social Capitalism itself is categorically distinguishable. One category is it being protective of free enterprise. The creation of wealth needs protection and law and order. A government military and police force are thus necessary. Another category is that it can promote free enterprise. The construction of railroads, highways and education has enabled more creation of economic wealth. Another category is that it competes against free enterprise. The use of solar energy in place carbon fuel is a prime example.

There have been social initiatives to replace carbon fuel with solar energy. In Eugene, Oregon, for instance, the Eugene Water and Electric Board offered to purchase electricity from home and building owners having solar panels to produce it. However, too many users of solar energy could result in not enough customers to whom the utility company needs to sell and maintain revenue above expenses.

The small town of Talent in southwestern Oregon even achieved a ninety-seven percent conversion to solar energy by means of a tax incentive as a 'cap and trade' enactment by legislature. It is testimonial to the influence of policies, but only on a small scale in becoming independent of the electrical grid of a nearby larger community. The larger community could eventually be in more need of revenue with the conversion of freer solar energy.

Suppose the utilities could purchase solar energy to sell as a cheaper means for more production of economic wealth. It would then be a promoter of free enterprise. However, there is then the option of producing for either social needs or free enterprise. If the electricity is cheaper from solar energy than from fossil fuels, then competitors using the cheaper electricity would have a competitive edge. However, an overall greater production of economic wealth would depend on its increase in demand according to a lower production cost. If there is no greater demand, then the utilities suffer from a loss of revenue.

What if local utilities of cities owned the solar panels and contracted with users of the solar energy for production of social wealth? It would be similar to the laissez faire and physiocratic economics of eighteenth century France whereby land owners were taxed in order for them to produce. Similarly, if utilities contracted with property owners, then the utilities could contract in turn with users of it to create social wealth. A difference in the physiocratic economics is it taxes the land owner to both finance government and initiate production of economic wealth, whereas this newer proposal is to contract with both home owners and producers for the creation of social wealth. However, what appears needed for its success is a cheaper solar energy than that of carbon fuels, and a way to maintain the same amount of distribution of capital among the citizenry.

A great amount of electricity is already produced by such natural means as dams, but some of it is still produced by carbon fuel. If local utilities contracted with local owners, the local communities could become more self-sufficient. Some larger supermarkets are already tending to become more self-sufficient by baking their own bread and self-producing other items on their shelves. The utility contract could allow more local production of products for supermarkets with regulative authority to ensure its reliability.

The utility contract would be categorized as a social investment, which has different consequences regarding purpose. If social investment is for protection of wealth, then it complements free enterprise. If it is for railroads and highways, then it promotes free enterprise. If it is to replace carbon fuel, then it counters free enterprise. The latter could still be more positive for free enterprise by contracting entrepreneurs for their help in the production of product. Oil companies, for instance, pump out of the ground about seven times more water than they do oil. Although most of it is too saline to drink or even use to raise crops, it could be purified to use wherever needed. Bone meal, for instance, contains such toxicity as mercury, as used in thermometers, and as can be eliminated from bones by simply baking them for fifty minutes. The collagen in the bones is then beneficial for healthy muscles, skin and hair.

A decisive factor of supply and demand economics other than competition is cost of production. Producing and selling more is generally more efficient for lower cost. However, the real cost of climate change is not money; it is commitment to the task at hand.

The task at hand is doable. Civilization developed from agriculture whereby food aplenty allowed the construction of great pyramids. The engineering and construction of canals and other irrigation systems, as Beaver Engineering, had previously coincided with the rise of civilization in the Mesopotamian Valley, and likely elsewhere. During the Bronze Age, three story buildings with running water and sewage from aqueducts and water reservoirs were built on such islands in the Mediterranean Sea as Crete. Romans later built an empire along with the construction of hundreds of miles of underground aqueducts and water reservoirs.

In the nineteenth century, railroads were built. In the twentieth century, highways consisted of long tunnels through mountainous areas. Astronauts in spaceships visited the moon. Those examples of social capitalism are complementary to either promoting free enterprise or at least non-competitive with it, but they are still viable evidence of what can be accomplished by us. What is actually needed is our agreement to commit. The financial part it is only needed for its facilitation. However, the facilitation process needs wisdom. If conditions of too hazardous hurricanes exist because of too much heat at the present time, and only a limited amount of sulfuric acid is used, then catastrophes could be prevented.

One such joint effort to commit to is Beaver Engineering. Water is the most central factor determining climate change. With it, food can be grown aplenty. Water reservoirs within forests could prevent forest fires. Holding back some of the river water and channeling it elsewhere would enable even more growth. Oil and gas is transported by trucks and railroad cars; they could just as well transport water, even if the water is kept in plastic barrels that do not become ocean trash, but are contained instead in greenhouses to help control a more moderate temperature.

The construction of the Grand Coulee dam in the state of Washington is another example of social cooperation. It allowed for farming along with the power to generate electricity to develop a prosperous community.

To the contrary, a severe drought in Afghanistan has resulted in farmers growing opium to survive, and to become controlled by drug dealers and terrorists, which has become a routine practice in Mexico and other less developed countries. The more effective long-term remedy is not a wall; it is the cooperation among countries to finance a healthier climate for a more productive life style.

Useful for such a remedy is a commitment to climate change remedies. A great number of people and organizations have already committed to it. The purchase of solar panels and electric cars are by individual choice. Such other remedies unaffordable by individuals, such as methods to abstract water from the atmosphere, require more of a social remedy of government and rules of large corporations for financing them.

Social finance has achieved economic success with the building of freeways and railroads for more transport of goods and services, thus increasing economic wealth. Public schools have also been a factor inasmuch as education and science provides knowledge for more choice that, in turn, inspires innovation for the advancement of products. Without science, it is not likely we would have television, telephones and so forth. Although scientists have not gotten the same wealth as larger entrepreneurs for their formulation of theory that has allowed inventions of countless products, they along with universities and public schools that enabled their education do deserve credit for their role instead of merely acknowledging the innovation of free enterprise as its role.

There are now many remedies to climate change on the open market. Solar panels have become affordable and promoted by electric and water utilities in some states. Electric cars are now a viable option to purchase, and they are promoted by such countries as China and Germany. Non-explosive lithium batteries to travel three hundred miles or more without recharging are now available. There is a small toy car for a three-year-old that is cheaper than other batteries, and it operates for seventeen hours before needing to be recharged.

Other remedies are too expensive for most individuals to purchase. Although alcohol has been used as a fuel throughout history, was an early source for engine combustion, and ethanol is now produced from corn in the Midwest, it along with electric batteries has been replaced with mostly gasoline engines. Although ethanol has less combustive energy than gasoline, it has a greater octane rating for more efficiency, except it is more difficult to ignite in colder weather, and its mixture with gasoline requires about ninety-five percent pure alcohol.

Biobutanol has an energy density close to that of gasoline, and it has a twenty-five cent better octane rating than gasoline, but it requires more chemical knowledge to effectively produce it as an economic alternative. It combines with gasoline and diesel fuels in allowing more water in the mixture than does ethanol. There are now technological claims that it can be produced from any green plants by solar energy and such fermentation bacteria from zebra waste.

There are methods to abstract water from the atmosphere even in arid climates, but they are neither affordable nor cost effective for most individuals. Although there are now tunnels through mountains and extensive roads and railroads built on public land for communities instead of individuals, the means of abstracting water from the atmosphere is not yet considered acceptable as a government investment. However, most of the sun's heat absorbed by Earth is from water. Although there is more surface water in the southern hemisphere for absorbing more heat when it is now both closer to and tilted towards the sun during summer, it is gradually reversing to the northern hemisphere. Because of less surface water, less overall heat by Earth will be absorbed, but the northern hemisphere still should become warmer in the summer and colder in the winter. As hot air absorbs more water, the overall atmosphere should become more humid in the summer from more rain and snow during the winter, but arid climates could also become even more arid from summer heat.

Natural climate change in addition to polluting the atmosphere with hydrocarbon fuels is more complex. What is needed is more investment in climatology to determine future effects of weather to determine remedies for such possible catastrophes as severe times of cold and heat, hurricanes, tornadoes, flooding, extensive forest fires, extreme drought and so forth. Physics and chemistry are also essential for knowledge, which itself provides more viable options to either counter or prepare for adverse effects of future weather.

NASA has been experimenting on closed systems for future space travel. Laser light can be used to extract hydrogen and oxygen from other materials for the use of fuel with water and air being maintained as byproducts. Such experiments could also be extended to the science of climatology regarding more advanced underground aqueducts and reservoirs.

Forestation instead of deforestation is critical to combating climate change, as plant life absorbs the carbon dioxide from the atmosphere for the benefit of animal life. Greenhouses for growing food could be beneficial on arid and semi-arid lands if water is economically available. Abstracting it from the atmosphere chemically, or from the use of alcohol fuels is expensive. Even the use of pure hydrogen as a fuel is dangerous and a threat to the upper ozone layer protecting us from too much ultraviolet light. More viable would be scientific projects using the produced water from oil companies. By government grants financed by such means as selling bonds to the public for it to share in the profit (as perhaps for retirement income and medical insurance), the water could be purchased from oil companies and purified. It need not only profit the oil companies along with the public, it could combat the corruption of growing opium and other drugs as well. By contracting with other countries, victims of corruption attempting to free from it could be offered the opportunity to become participants of an experimental development of a greenhouse development of arid lands that are otherwise unlivable to most of us Moreover, although the development could compete with present development, the production by the otherwise poor would increase demand for both the consumption and production of more overall wealth.

Such a project could be carried out on several levels. On a state level, the semi-arid land in the eastern parts of Washington, Oregon and California could be developed. On a global level, the World Bank of the United Nations could contract with countries of the Sahara Desert, Mexico, Afghanistan and so forth for the prospect of both more peaceful conditions and prosperity at large.

As of now, the conditions of Climate Change by the use of carbon fuel needs to be in a way it does not pollute the atmosphere. Even the use of combining oxygen and hydrogen as a fuel with its byproduct being water can be harmful by depleting the upper ozone layer of heavy oxygen that protects us from too much energetic ultraviolet radiation of sunlight to cause skin cancer instead of only creating vitamin D for human health. In this respect, there is also a nitrogen cycle to consider. Air contains a large amount of nitrogen that is only useful as fertilizer for plant life if converted by worms, bacteria or scientific method in combining the nitrogen with hydrogen, as in the form of ammonia, $NH_3$, but the atmosphere absorbs oxygen of the high energy use of hydrogen oxygen fuel in allowing the hydrogen to absorb some of the heavy oxygen of the ozone layer instead.

Water is both essential and hazardous to life. We tend to populate nearer to rivers and lakes contrary to arid and semi-arid environments. Flooding does result in the destruction of property and loss of life. Although there have been attempts to control the weather, as by filling the atmosphere with chemicals to cause more rain, flooding from one hurricane can supply enough water to fill billions of swimming pools. Simply put, the atmosphere is too large for us to directly control its natural effects. On the other hand, massive 'beaver-engineering' is both a secondary and productive means of controlling the water supply.

'Beaver-engineering' has a successful history. The Romans built a huge empire along with an elaborate structure of miles and miles of mostly underground aqueducts and reservoirs. The construction of the Grand Coulee dam in the state of Washington provides electricity along with a prosperous farming community. Countless dams and reservoirs are likewise beneficial here and there. Extracting water from more humid air to allow more natural flow along with water usage in arid regions could also be beneficial.

More beaver engineering could indeed be beneficial. Dust from the Sahara Desert of Africa reaching Florida since the 1970s has attributed to the destruction of coral reefs. The Sahara Desert is more than three thousand miles from near the Red Sea to near the Atlantic Ocean. It is the most arid region of Earth's surface, but there are underground flows of water from the Atlas Mountains, and other mountainous areas, that provide flourishing oasis here and there.

The main population of Egypt has flourished beside the Nile River, but the Nile Valley could become flooded by the rise of sea levels from global warming. Storing water in the part of the Sahara Desert in Egypt, similar to the Roman aqueducts and reservoirs, could be an effective counter. Moreover, although the desert is hot and dry, sunlight and dry trade winds blowing southwest towards the equator are plentiful for the developmental use of solar energy. They could be used to tunnel into the desert whereby water could be collected, transported and stored with more efficiency with productive use, as for underground-greenhouse-gardens protected from the sandy wind of the desert. Sturdy dome structures atop the soil could also counter the destructiveness of the wind, as by slowing it down and causing it to flow higher.

Algeria, with its populated area bordering the Mediterranean Sea, has invested in solar energy of sunlight and wind. It also supplies Europe with a large amount of natural gas. Although the natural gas can pollute the atmosphere with both too much hydrogen, it would not be a pollutant if used in a confined manner, as underground or within a sturdy enough structure. If controlled with underground use, the hydrogen and carbon of the natural gas, $H_4C$, combined with nitrogen and oxygen of the air could be converted to water and a fertilized form of nitrogen for plant growth. The plant growth, in turn, would resupply the atmosphere with oxygen and nitrogen. Moreover, although excess hydrogen in the atmosphere can contribute to global warming, as water absorbing heat, hydrogen can also be converted to helium, which is already done for commercial purposes. The helium could then be used for solar powered blimps to transport water to desert greenhouses and also transport products from those greenhouses to wherever needed.

Such investments in the future could pay for themselves in the present. Economic wealth is essentially product; money is merely a means of credit to facilitate such investment. More food, water and livable environment could result in a fair distribution of wealth for the promotion of peace and prosperity. As in Afghanistan where farmers have taken to grow opium because of it being able to grow in the arid climate that nutritional crops are now unable to do, more future drought will result in economic revolt for the need of survival.

The investment could be shared, as in analogy to a stock exchange, whereby the elderly could receive a retirement income. If there are fewer products in the future, then inflation reduces retirement income whereby our grandchildren become more in debt instead of having products aplenty to spend their money on. Prosperity is thus achieved by investing in the future, whether by free enterprise or by government. The latter could be more effective for environmental concern in the sense water along with air is essential to life but too plentiful for economic value, and to be an economic burden to industrial pollution. Politically, there is the need to overcome "me first".

In nature, there already exists cycles of change. In the far western continental states, for instance, there is about a twenty-year cycle between drought and more rain. An extreme rainy period occurs in between the drought years. Such cycles that now occur are not new; what is new is the increase to the extreme for more severe effects. Along with successive drought and extreme flooding are more frequent and more severe hurricanes and tornadoes, melting of glaciers, rising sea levels, ocean acidity, dust storms, more spread of such diseases associated with malaria fever and salmonella outbreaks, and a decrease in both marine and animal life, including more human deaths because of starvation and other effects due to climate change.

These results are now the carbon footprint of the atmosphere from our excessive use of hydrocarbon fuels. There is more usable energy in the atmosphere, but it is more uncontrollable, as evident of the increase in more natural disasters related to climate change. To counter this change, we can build sturdier structures to withstand it, pollute less, and clean up the mess we create, and we could find ways to control and use the atmospheric energy in less harmful ways.

The energy in the atmosphere can also be tapped. Besides wind and photoelectric cells for mechanical and electrical power, carbon and water can be recycled for commercial use, as they are vital parts of the food chain. Carbon itself is naturally produced in countless forms. It can be crystalline in the form of diamonds and graphite. Diamonds are more of an insulator of heat and electricity; graphite is ideal for conducting heat and electricity and can be used as an electrode. Russia, China, Turkey, India, Madagascar, Canada and Mexico are the main nations producing graphite, but it is now more commercially produced by heating the coke of petroleum by means of electricity. Such granite as charcoal can be produced effectively by heating such vegetarian waste as wood with enough heat and time in a container separating it from oxygen, which would result in combustion and polluting the atmosphere with carbon dioxide.

If we filled the atmosphere with giant blimps, as unmanned computerized drones electrically powered by the sun and wind, they could use the atmospheric energy for more productive use instead of more hazardous effects. For instance, they could extract water and carbon from the atmosphere and transport it to where it is needed for agriculture and so forth. It would take an enormous number of blimps to reverse global warming, but the effort could be rewarding both economically and environmentally. If located most efficiently, as to be able to extract water from areas of greater humidity, as is the equator. By using the natural directions of the winds, the atmosphere could become controlled by commercial use instead of it remaining uncontrollable. Moreover, enough giant blimps in the sky might provide a superhighway for the travel above water for not increasing the sea level, and for a network of fishing, gaming and whatever.

Blimps are not a total solution to climate change, but they could still be part of the solution.

Other remedies could entail better use of material resources. As glaciers continue to melt, rising sea levels could be prevented by building reservoirs to hold more water. The downstream flow of fresh water from the mountains to the oceans could be slowed for less water waste. Reservoirs along with storm forecasts could also regulate the flow of water in preventing flooding from too rapid change in the weather, as in the early melting of winter snow.

At NASA there has been scientific effort to perfect a natural carbon cycle for future travel in space. As hydrocarbons, air and water are consumed and converted to $CO_2$ and methane gas of carbon and hydrogen, $CH_4$. Indicated as the most efficient means of recycling the $CO_2$ and $CH_4$ back to air and water is the use of different light frequencies of laser light.

Here on Earth, the scientific conversion can be combined with solar and other natural resources. Solar wind and light can be used to separate water into hydrogen and oxygen. The hydrogen alone can be used as fuel with air to create energy with a byproduct of water. Computerized blimps, as giant drones, can transport the hydrogen from the equator while decreasing the potential magnitude of hurricanes with the use of wind power along with sunlight energy. (Although the hydrogen can be explosive, it explodes mainly up instead of down because of it being the lightest of the elements.)

The means of accomplishment are available. They just need to be technically understood in the manner of beaver engineering. Beavers create dams and deeper reservoirs to maintain greater water supply. The climate change solution is similar; it is just a lot more technical and complex. It is more technical in the sense more scientific study is needed to determine the impact of feasible solutions and how they can be efficiently implemented. It is more complex in the sense different areas of impact are conditional to the nature of their terrains. Blimps following the Atlantic winds from the equator into the Gulf of Mexico can more easily serve the deserts of Mexico. Water can more easily be preserved in the states of California, Oregon and Washington during increased rainfall. Deeper reservoirs might be created in the mountains of California with the use of solar energy that could also be continually used to create an electric grid of solar batteries that, in turn, are helpful in the construction process. Excess snow and water in the Cascades of Oregon could be diverted to fill the countless wells that already exist east of the Cascades. Alcohol or hydrogen-oxygen fuel can be substituted for gasoline for water as a byproduct. Excess water from the Great Lakes could be channeled all the way to Arizona and New Mexico. These measures might even be needed in order to prevent future flooding conditions in preparing for a better future.

The social effort could even promote free enterprise. Surface water and more humid air maintain more heat. Large enough facilities to use the energy of sunlight to decompose the air could render more economic wealth of product. The air not only contains oxygen, water, carbon and nitrogen; it contains such trace elements as helium, which can be produced by separating liquefied air or natural gas into individual components. Socially capitalizing on such treasury is an economic means of creating both economic wealth and controlling climate change. It might even employ the homeless in combating it and for it to help produce more food and shelter for long use of carbon being less pollutant.

In retrospect, as computerized robots are gradually replacing manual labor, the more productive result now requires more educated users of the robots for using them in a way that promotes both economic and social wealth for a healthier world in which to live along with world peace and prosperity.

www.ingramcontent.com/pod-product-compliance
Lightning Source LLC
Chambersburg PA
CBHW030951240526
45463CB00016B/2336